Laws and Disorders

Laws and Disorders

A Law-Breaking Guide to Real but
Bizarre Laws from Over the Centuries

Richard De'ath

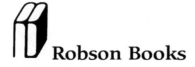

Robson Books

This paperback edition published in 1999 by Robson Books, 10 Blenheim Court, Brewery Road, London N7 9NT

First published in hardback in Great Britain as *Sod's Law* by Robson Books Ltd.

A member of the Chrysalis Group plc

Copyright © 1995 Richard De'ath

Book design by Harold King

The right of Richard De'ath to be identified as author of this work has been asserted by him in accordance with the Copyright, Designs and Patent Act 1988

British Library Cataloguing in Publication Data
A catalogue record for this title is available from the British Library

ISBN 1 86105 295 2

Printed and bound in Great Britain by Creative Print and Design Wales, Ebbw Vale

It ain't no sin if you crack
a few laws now and then,
just so long as you don't break any.

MAE WEST

Contents

$\mathfrak{I}$NTRODUCTION

The expression 'Sod's Law' is one in everyday use – my family and friends use it regularly as I suspect most of you do, too. It is normally employed to describe that kind of inevitable force in nature which causes a piece of bread to always land on the buttered side; rain to fall mostly at weekends; and the telephone to ring the very moment you step into the bath. The term is, in fact, both ancient and widespread: Socrates, for example, in one of his *Dialogues* referred to the 'general cussedness of things' and in Ireland it has been known for centuries as Murphy's Law. Across the Atlantic, the same thing is called by the Americans Finagle's Law, while the French habitually use the expression *la loi d'emmerdement maximum* to describe the experience. I have even heard it referred to on occasions as the Buggeration Factor.

The 'formulation' of this law is, though, uncertain and the statements about it that I have come across are many, varied and frequently crude. Which is the very reason why I have appropriated the term as the title for this book although it is actually about some much more specific, if equally curious, laws. For just as humanity has for years puzzled over the discrepancies of Sod's Law, in life the world's lawmakers have also been busy creating a whole slew of statutes, ordinances and rules which similarly defy description. And it is the strangest, most bizarre and sometimes, frankly, almost unbelievable of these which I have gathered together from the four corners of the globe in the following pages.

Another familiar exclamation frequently heard from people when they are confronted by infuriating pieces of bureaucracy is, 'There should be a law against it!' Well, the evidence suggests to me that there probably has been. For as Alexander Woollcott remarked, 'All the things I like to do are either illegal or immoral or fattening,' and the fact is undeniable that quite a number of those in authority have been taking the aphorism quite literally ever since. For wherever you choose to look, there has almost certainly been a lawmaker tinkering with the more absurd and obscure elements of life.

Who, for instance, could not help wondering at the minds that devised a rule which fined hairdressers who ate garlic during working hours? Which might imprison goats for grazing on other people's properties? Or could send a couple to a prison cell for the night who accidently sound the horn of a car in which they are making love? Perhaps even more curious, that a legislator could sit down and write: 'Sacrificing accuracy somewhat recklessly for the sake of brevity, I am tempted to say that the object of the action is to determine which of these two bodies, if either, is the other, and, if not, whether either; and if so which, is another corporate body of the same name, or if not in fact such third body, is identical with it.'

But the proof of such things is to be found on page after page of the world's statute books – and though a good many were introduced years ago and have probably not been implemented for generations, they have just as certainly never been repealed. Every one of the weird and wonderful laws in this book still exists.

It will probably come as a surprise to no one that by far the largest number of these very odd laws emanate from the nation that loves litigation above all others – the United States; or that the topics most subjected to international legislation have been love, sex and animals. In some of the cases, it seems amazing that any legislator would have taken the time and trouble to even formulate the laws, let alone get them incorporated onto the statute books.

In this context, I am reminded of the story of a certain American legislator who became so fed up with the cursory perusal that his colleagues gave to the bills passing through their assembly that he took the matter into his own hands. In 1967, quite straight-faced, he introduced a bill which commended a man then very much in the news. The wording ran, 'Mr Albert DeSalvo – in acknowledgement of his outstanding work in population control.'

I find it almost as incredible as anything that follows in these pages to record that that bill was passed unanimously – and despite the fact that DeSalvo was then on trial charged with murdering 13 women. For he was the infamous 'Boston Strangler'.

1

ADAM v EVE

The Unlikely Trials
Of Matrimony

The American state of Texas is famous for its tall stories about things there being bigger and better than anywhere else in the world. To that could be added the fact it is also a place which still enshrines one of the most bizarre laws about courting. Indeed, it was hearing all about this statute while visiting the USA that gave me the idea for this book.

The law operates in the small town of Anson in west central Texas, not far from the bustling, oil-refining city of Abilene. Anson's main claim to fame – apart from the curious law in question – is for playing host to the annual 'Cowboys' Christmas Party'. But it is also the only town in the world where dancing is effectively banned. For more than 50 years, a local ordinance has not only forbidden public dances but also the consumption of alcohol, 'because dancing leads to drunkenness, debauchery, adultery, divorce and unwanted pregnancies'.

However, after years of being notorious for its aversion to the waltz and the foxtrot – let alone the horrors of rock 'n' roll – Anson has recently seen the emergence of an opposition group calling itself Footloose, who want to change the law. This cross-section of teenagers and young married couples believe the ban that keeps the town dry and declares dancing a sin, actually represents a threat to normal friendships between the sexes. As a member of Footloose insisted: 'A nice dance now and then – what's wrong with that? This repression is having the wrong effect. Why, five girls got pregnant only last year. And do you know where most of these goings-on happened? In the back seats of cars in the parking lot behind the church!'

Yet the city fathers remain unmoved, one of their number declaring after a recent meeting: 'A dance is the only place where a man can freely handle another man's wife and I have seen some pretty good fights if a man holds her too tight. There have even been some killings – which was why the ordinance was passed and why it should stay in force.'

Whatever the future holds, Anson has a well earned reputation as 'the town out of step with the world'. But as this book will reveal, it is also far from being the only place still to uphold the weirdest laws where love, courtship and marriage are concerned . . .

WAGES OF SIN

Pilots who served in the Italian Air Force during the Second World War were subjected to a code of conduct instituted by the dictator Mussolini which forbade them from making advances to girls in public places. Although the ruling is technically redundant now in the modern state of Italy, one wartime pilot has found this singular law coming back to punish him. Calogero Lo Ricco, from Messina in Sicily, was given a suspended three-month sentence in 1941 and now stands to lose his veteran's pension because a Treasury official has implemented the wartime ruling and demanded the repayment of the £5,700 Calogero has drawn in the intervening years. And his crime? Giving a woman a little kiss on the cheek at her front door – the self-same woman who has been his wife for fifty years!

ROMEOS PROHIBITED

The old tradition of serenading a girl from beneath her balcony, which Shakespeare immortalized in *Romeo and Juliet*, is not so kindly looked upon in the American city of Boston, Massachusetts. For an old city ordinance says that 'no husband or lover may sing to the object of his affections at night outside her bedroom window' – *unless* he has a special licence obtained from the mayor's office.

KISS OF DEATH

The laws about public displays of affection are very severe in Abu
Dhabi in the United Arab Emirates. The simple act of putting an
arm around a woman or giving her a gentle kiss on the cheek
constitutes 'an action that could be harmful to the public good'
says the law – and a persistent lover runs the risk of being
sentenced to death as the price for his infatuation.

NO MATCH

Dating and matchmaking agencies which are so popular in the
West have certain restrictions in Chinese society, according to a
recent piece of legislation from the China State Council. A report
about this ruling in the daily newspaper, *Ta Kung Pao* in February
1995 stated that 'a ban has been ordered on matchmaking
companies offering overseas marriages for Chinese citizens.'

SEX POLICE

In Peking, China's bustling capital city, the green-uniformed
officers of the Public Security Bureau (PSB) – better known as the

'Sex Police' – have the power to arrest any foreign visitor for what is described euphemistically as 'insulting' a Chinese woman or girl. More specifically, this means it is against the law for male tourists to take Chinese women to their hotel bedrooms for sex – this is considered an 'insult' whether the girl is a prostitute or not – although the rules make no mention of intercourse occurring in any other room or even in hotel lifts. These lifts have, apparently, become popular rendezvous spots in recent years because of their tendency to break down with unerring regularity between floors.

FLIRTING BAN

Abilene, in west Texas, USA, is still governed by a law about flirting that has been on the state books since the early years of this century. This makes it illegal for anyone to 'ply the avocation of flirt or masher'. The quaint rule continues: 'It shall further be unlawful for any man to stare at or make googoo eyes at, or in any other manner look at or make remarks to or concerning, or cough or whistle at, or do any other act to attract the attention of any women upon or travelling along any of the sidewalks, streets, public ways of the city of Abilene with an intent or in a manner calculated to annoy such a woman.'

PUTTING UP A GOOD FRONT

In a number of settlements in the Gobi region of Mongolia, an old law requires that women should wear a wrap at least nine yards long, but which leaves their breasts exposed. This curious rule actually dates from the Middle Ages when the rulers of the wandering tribes of Mongols – forever on their guard against assassins – ordered all females to bear their bosoms, 'so there would be no mistaking them for killers disguised as women'.

RETURN TO SENDER

In the South American country of Ecuador, virginity in young girls is very highly valued. Pre-marital sex is frowned on by a number of the country's long-established laws. One of the oldest of these declares that a new husband who discovers his bride is not a virgin, 'may return her to her parents and consider himself unmarried from that day forward'.

LEARNING THE HARD WAY

The cost of wedded bliss can be high for the lovelorn in the state of Bauchi in northern Nigeria. For here any man who wishes to marry a young bride under the age of 15 risks a fine of 1,000 naira (about £800) or six months in jail – as do the girl's parents or guardians if they consent to the marriage. The reason for this tough punishment is quite simple – the man is 'interrupting the girl's education'.

LEWDNESS LAW

Ashland, a picturesque American city close to the Kentucky State boundary with West Virginia, is strict about the type of women that a resident is allowed to have living under his roof. For according to a statute laid down over a hundred years ago, 'No person shall knowingly keep or harbour at his or her house within the city limits any woman of ill-repute, lewd character or a common prostitute – other than a wife, mother or sister.'

PAINTING THE TOWN

Couples who either bathe in the nude or make love in the open air anywhere in the locality of Georgetown in Guyana, can suffer a very salutary punishment because of a law that has been on the statute books since 1920.

They will be promptly arrested, swiftly covered with a coat of bright red paint, and then forced to walk home revealing their shame for everyone to see.

Persistent offenders risk an even more degrading punishment – after being painted they will be 'attached to an ass and taken on a tour of the area' before facing a heavy fine or even imprisonment.

NAVY PINCH

It is not only in Italy that the law tends to turn a blind eye to men patting or pinching girls on the bottom. The huge American seaport of Norfolk, Virginia – famous for years as the headquarters of the US Atlantic fleet – still has an old law on the statute books that allows this activity to go on unhindered. But with one basic difference, however. Here it is the *women* who can pat an attractive male behind with impunity – a man who tries to do the same to a passing female runs the risk of a fine of $150 or up to 60 days in prison.

HONK AND WAIT

Lovers could do a lot worse than visit the hospitable little US town with the romantic French name of Coeur d'Alene near Spokane in Idaho. For this community nestling in the foothills of the Bitterroot Range believes in letting lovers make love – even if they happen to do it in a parked car. An ordinance passed twenty years ago forbids any law officer from disturbing couples at play. If he has any reason to believe that public decency might be offended, then his instructions are clear. The law says he must pull up near the vehicle, honk his horn three times, 'and then wait two minutes before getting out of his patrol car to investigate'.

THE PRICE OF MARRIAGE

Couples considering marriage on the beautiful island of Papua, New Guinea, off the northern coast of Australia, are still bound by a curious dowry law which has never been repealed. Women are highly regarded here and a man is expected to pay the equivalent of £200, five pigs and one bird for a virgin bride. The dowry changes to half that sum, two pigs and one bird for a widower or divorced women. Only after a Papuan woman has been married twice does her value really plummet. For, says the local law, 'she is of no commercial value'.

CONFETTI BAN

Couples who have decided to go to the altar should avoid getting married in Wichita, the capital of Kansas in the United States. For, under an ordinance which has been on the statute books for the past half-century, it is against the law to mark the happy event with the traditional confetti-throwing ceremony. This is what some obviously gloomy city fathers had written into local law all those years ago: 'That it shall be unlawful for any person to throw upon or against another person in the city of Wichita, any confetti or similar preparation or to throw same about in any street or public building or place in said city. It is further made unlawful for any person to throw as aforesaid any flour, talcum powder, rice or other substance or preparations for the purpose of annoying or harassing others.'

WORDS OF LOVE

Many words are exchanged between couples while making love – from the tenderest of endearments to the most terrible profanities. In the little town of Willowdale, in Oregon, USA, the lawmakers actually drew up an ordinance about this very thing almost a century ago. They decided it was an act punishable by a fine if a husband 'cursed or swore while consummating the joys of married life'. Wives, on the other hand, were free to use any language they chose – dependent, no doubt, on their partner's performance!

SHOTGUN WEDDINGS

There are good reasons why the law has forbidden the firing of any weapons during wedding ceremonies throughout the American state of Pennsylvania. In the wilder years of the past, marriages were often drunken affairs where tempers frayed and arguments were settled with guns. Hence the introduction of a state-wide ban that is still on the statute books, that rules that during a marriage ceremony 'there may be no shooting of rifles, pistols or cannons under any circumstances'.

EVERY HAIR ON HER HEAD

A man's ownership of his wife even extended to her hair according to a nineteenth-century law which was enacted in the American state of Michigan and has not yet been deleted from the statute books. This law maintained that after her marriage a woman's hair 'rightfully belonged' to her husband and she even had to seek his permission to get it cut.

MOTHER IN THE LAWS

For over a hundred years husbands living in Wichita in the heart of Kansas, USA have enjoyed a special immunity where difficult mothers-in-law are concerned. Because according to an ordinance brought in shortly after the rapid growth of the city from a cow town and rail hub in 1872, a man is not obliged to be pleasant to his wife's mother. Such behaviour is also not admissible in any case for divorce which his wife might subsequently initiate.

SILENCE IS BEHOLDEN

Men returning home late to their wives or partners in London could be in a tricky situation if they receive a frosty reception and then allow their tempers to get the better of them. For ever since the seventeenth century, a statute has been in existence in the capital that limits violence to cohabiting women. 'Wife beating is forbidden in London after 9 o'clock in the evening,' it states, 'because of the noise.'

BED-RIDDENCE

The city of Lebanon in Kentucky, USA, which is the location of one of America's national cemeteries, also has a unique law in place about resting in peace at home in bed. Here an old statute forbids any man who suffers from that age-old problem of a wife with cold feet who will insist upon putting them on his back, from pushing her out of bed. It is against the law – and any wife who files a complaint about this breach of the peace can have her man fined or even locked up for a week. Which might, of course, be a relief if it spares him a few nights of cold feet!

THE GENTLE TOUCH

Illicit relationships are often punished by brutal strokes of the lash in the Arab state of Abu Dhabi. In one famous instance, however, a foreign national, a woman from Sri Lanka who had been convicted of adultery, found herself instead sentenced to be whipped one hundred times ... but in 'a gentle manner,' to quote the court ruling. So she was beaten with the stem of a date-palm leaf.

THE PRICE OF LOVE

A curious ruling in force in the largest South African city, Johannesburg, is believed to date back to the 1880s when the place was developing rapidly as the centre of the Transvaal gold-mining region. This permitted a woman to charge her husband a fee for making love, though only what was considered 'a reasonable price'. Though this 'price of love' has never been firmly established, one magistrate who ruled on a case in 1929 gave a classic definition which has been frequently quoted. 'The bed is the poor man's opera,' he said. 'For a poor man, however, a charge of 10 rand a ticket might put the show beyond the realms of popular entertainment.

WIFE BEATING

Time has almost stood still in Jasper, the lovely old southern town in Alabama whose very name still smacks of the past. One law that remains is certainly from a different age and permits the menfolk to beat their womenfolk if they think they have stepped out of line. Says the appropriate section: 'Since a husband of this town is held responsible for the behaviour of his wife, he may punish her for any misbehaviour and has the legal right to chastise her with a stick. This stick may be no larger around than the husband's thumb.'

DOUBLE BLESSING

Bigamy is, of course, a well-known offence, and the punishments for committing it range from terms of imprisonment to the death sentence in some of the more repressive nations. The Hungarians, however, have certainly the strangest law of all. Under a current ruling any man who has married for a second time without properly divorcing his first wife may be sentenced to support *both* women – and also to live with them both under the same roof.

MATE GUARD

A curious form of chaperoning for married women is still part of the law in the peaceful American state of Virginia. This takes the form of an old ordinance which dates back to the pioneer days – yet it has still not been removed from the statute books. In effect it says that no married woman may walk out alone on a Sunday unless she is 'properly' accompanied: ie, that she is followed by her husband 'at a distance of not more than twenty paces at any time', carrying a weapon. Though today's police force might object to the sight of hundreds of men walking around with guns at the ready – as this law permits – it was implemented at a time when there were rather more Indians on the prowl trying to take captive the wives of settlers than there are nowadays.

BURNED UP

The English wife who recently took such pleasure in destroying her unfaithful husband's clothes would have actually had the law on her side if she happened to live in Ohio, USA. Because throughout the state a statute has long been in place to the effect that a wife may burn her husband's old clothing 'if they are unpleasant to her' and there is also nothing to stop her throwing out any of his sportswear or sporting equipment.

THE PARTING OF THE FRUITS

Lawyers in Louisiana in the Deep South of the United States have even gone so far as to draw up legislation to cover what happens to any produce on a couple's piece of land when they decide to get divorced. The facts are these: 'The fruits hanging by the roots on the lands belonging separately to either the husband or the wife, at the time of the dissolution of the marriage, are to be equally divided between the husband and the wife.'

MOTHER OUTLAW

Jokes about interfering mothers-in-law have a special relevance in the city of Kaunas in Lithuania. Because here many years ago the local authorities, aware of the fact that many mothers-in-law actually live with their daughters and sons-in-law, put a unique law into effect. This recognized that in the tiny homes of most Lithuanians, room space is at a premium and for husbands and wives to find a little privacy for love-making was virtually impossible under normal circumstances. So they made it lawful for a husband to ban his mother-in-law from the house for several hours if he had *l'amour* on his mind! Curiously, the law did not insist that the husband must explain his actions to the older woman – nor did it give the same power to the wife if her mother-in-law happened to live with the couple.

PAINFUL SEPARATION

Another Lithuanian town, Panevezys, has an even stranger law in force which covers the grounds on which a man may divorce his wife. These include the predictable ones of adultery or desertion – though being a poor housekeeper or bad cook are also acceptable reasons in the local court. However, the lawmaker who drew up this statute in the eighteenth century made it extremely difficult for a wife to free herself from a cruel or adulterous husband. For according to the statute, her only grounds for a separation were if her husband had 'contracted boils on his genitals'.

SUICIDE BIDS

Britain is the only country in the world where an old law decrees that if two people agree to commit suicide together and only one is successful, the survivor is guilty of murder. In 1985, the topic also made news in Paris when a man was charged in court under a curious French variation. He was author Yves Le Bonniec, who was fined 10,000 francs after being found guilty of 'non-assistance' of a person in danger. He had failed to do anything to help the victim despite receiving two letters from him. The book M Le Bonniec had written was a do-it-yourself suicide guide.

A GAP IN THE LAW

Some very unusual items of property have been the centre of dispute in divorce proceedings. Husbands and wives have demanded that a whole range of personal items from furniture to pets and even cuddly toys should be made over to them in court settlements – but in New York a law which has only been on the statute books for the past thirty years is arguably the most unusual. For this specifies that there is one item no man may demand of his ex-partner – her false teeth. In the states of Louisiana and Vermont, it is also against the law for anyone to take a bankrupt man or woman's false teeth in payment of part of the debt.

TICKET TO RIDE

Married couples living in the little American town of Corning, Iowa, have always had second thoughts before going out in the car, all because of an antiquated turn of-the-century rule. This says that it is breaking the law for a man to ask any woman, whether she be his wife or a single girl, to get into his automobile. But if he does so – says that old piece of legislation – then he is liable to be charged with solicitation.

2
BAD TASTE

Indigestible Facts About
Food and Drink

Greengrocers all over Europe have recently become the latest shopkeepers to find themselves subjected to some very strange new Euro-rules introduced by the bureaucrats of Brussels. The first of these EU rules covering fruit and vegetables insisted that cucumbers had to be smooth and banned from sale any that were 'knobbly'. Then it was the turn of carrots – they are now to be classified as fruit and not vegetables – followed by chilli peppers 'which must be sold in pairs'. More ridiculous still – all bananas now have to be at least five and a half inches long and 'not too bent'.

What has been described as 'the last strawb' was the ruling issued in 1995 that all strawberries must be 'heart-shaped and 85 per cent red'. Strawberries that failed either of these criteria – or worse still, grew 'too square' – must not be offered for sale. As one London fruit wholesaler commented, 'These are crazy rules and regulations – they can't change the shape of fruit and determine the course of nature!' But breaking the rules can still land the offender with a £5,000 fine.

However, fruit and vegetables are not the only comestibles to be subject to 'fruit-and-nut case bureaucracy' as one British newspaper light-heartedly described these latest laws. There are quite a number of others relating to food and drink to be found all over the world ...

CANNED DOWN

Opening a tin of food of any kind can often be a bit of a trial. But it is not a subject that has attracted much attention from the lawmakers, except in the curiously named community of Spades in Indiana, USA. There a rule was laid down in 1894 that it was illegal to attempt to open a tin by shooting at it with a revolver. The penalty for ignoring this law could be as high as three months in the can.

HAGGIS AWA'!

The famous Scottish delicacy of haggis which is made from a sheep's heart, liver and lungs minced with onion, oatmeal, suet, spice, salt and pepper, boiled in the animal's stomach, has not always found an easy entry into foreign countries because of its strange composition. Brazil has perhaps the oddest rule for allowing the haggis to be imported into the nation – for there it is categorized not as a foodstuff but 'unscheduled horticulture fertilizer'.

SKINNED AROUND

The manufacturers of sausages in the United States were recently faced with the introduction of a new piece of legislation which, once again, proved to be a triumph for the lawmaker's art of obscuration. It dealt with the process of removing the casings from sausages, and stated, in part: 'In a sausage-skinning machine, means for rotating a sausage about its longitudinal axis, means for holding a part of the skin against rotative movement with the sausage to cause said skin to be torn off said sausage circumferentially, and means for simultaneously moving said sausage endwise with respect to said holding means, said rotating, holding and moving means being operatively related to one another to cause said skin to be torn off and stripped from the sausage helically.'

LIE-DOWN FOOD

Tasmania in Australia has shown a lot of concern for the welfare of customers using its restaurants and bars. For the past ten years a local rule has insisted that no food may be served in any establishment that is not provided with wheelchairs and a stretcher.

SLURPING SOUP

Listening to someone eating soup noisily is an unpleasant experience for any diner to have to endure. In New Jersey, USA, the habit actually resulted in the making of a law that has never been rescinded. No person, it says, may slurp their soup in a public restaurant 'to the annoyance of other customers' without running the risk of being arrested and fined. Persistent offenders may even end up well and truly in the soup by getting a jail sentence.

CARROTS FOR SEX

The qualities of carrots have been debated by nutritionists and government agencies for years. During the Second World War, for instance, carrots were said to be part of the staple diet of RAF pilots thus enabling them to 'see in the dark', while actually keeping even darker the great British secret weapon – radar – from the Germans. In the Indian state of Rajasthan, however, carrot seeds have a rather different purpose: the seeds are used in trying to stem a tide of unwanted pregnancies. For there the authorities have passed a law which requires women to eat the seeds as a contraceptive.

DEEP FRIED

The popular fish and chip shop was always in danger of getting into hot oil with British law until the outbreak of the Second World War. According to the statute books, fish frying had for years been officially classified with a number of other occupations as an 'offensive trade'. But as a result of new legislation introduced in October 1940, while the nation was at war with Nazi Germany and the provision of food for the population was of paramount importance, the nation's fish and chip shop proprietors were withdrawn from the same category as the 'blood-boilers and gut-scrapers'.

SUNDAY FLAVOUR

Even ice-cream has run foul of authority in a number of countries. In Italy, for example, certain small communities have laws governing its sale on Sundays, while in America the ice-cream soda should not be sold at all on the Sabbath in the town of Evanston, close to Chicago. This statute was introduced in 1882 and immediately raised a furore amongst ice-cream lovers. A local drug-store owner, William C Garwood, thought he had found a way round this by calling the drink a 'Sunday' – but he had reckoned without the local church leaders who objected to this association with the holy day. After a heated exchange, both sides agreed to cool down: and hereafter Mr Garwood's invention has been known as a 'Sundae'.

ICE-CREAM CARRIER

There are probably any number of ways of carrying ice-creams – though no one has yet invented a way to prevent them dripping. Yet the lawmakers in the city of Lexington in Kentucky, USA, must have given the matter some thought and then put on their statute books one particular way in which an ice-cream cone was not to be carried in their community. In the pocket.

CANDY BAN

It is tough having a sweet tooth in the town of Salem, West Virginia, on a Sunday. Because an old rule going back to the eighteenth century forbids anyone from eating 'all sweetmeats' or candy for the hour and a half before the evening church service begins. And this same ruling also threatens any shopkeeper with a stiff fine if he sells sweets to a child in the same period. After church, there is nothing to prevent anyone gorging himself.

FAGGED OUT

Candy cigarettes hardly seem like something the lawmakers would take a strong exception to – yet they have done in North Dakota, USA, where legislation was brought to bear on them a few years ago. Because a pressure group believed that eating these sweetmeats was the first step towards a child taking up smoking, a rule was introduced onto the statute books that now bans the sale of them anywhere in the state.

ICE-CREAM PRIVILEGE

Picturesque Ocean Beach in New York has a number of tough anti-litter laws about the carrying of open containers of food, all of which are aimed at keeping the streets clean. A recent case made front-page news when three tourists were charged with eating in public. One man was chewing a chocolate biscuit, a second was munching a piece of cake and a girl with them was drinking water from a paper cup. When the three counter-claimed that lots of people all around them were eating ice-creams at the time, it was pointed out that this particular item of food was specifically exempted under a 60-year-old local ordinance.

NUTS (ABOUND)

Peanuts, those favourite snacks sometimes called monkey-nuts, gave rise to an extraordinary piece of legislative jargon in 1947. The nuts, which belong to the family *Leguminosae* and are borne on stalks after the death of the flower and bury themselves in the earth to ripen, are also categorized as ground-nuts. In 1947, a British government project for mass-cultivation in Tanganyika known as 'The Ground-Nut Scheme' turned into a fiasco losing between £30 and £40 million in five years. But it did leave as a legacy this piece of nutty law as a tribute to the lawmaker's art of obscuration: 'In the Nuts (unground) (other than ground-nuts) Order, the expression nuts shall have reference to such nuts, other than ground-nuts, as would but for this amending Order not qualify as nuts (unground) (other than ground-nuts) by reason of their being nuts (unground).'

PEANUT BATTER

The peanut was also not so popular with the city fathers of Springfield, Illinois, where Abraham Lincoln once lived, practised law and now lies buried. Fed up with all the shells which were constantly being found beneath the pews in churches, they banned the eating of these nuts in all the city's places of worship on Sundays. Any other day of the week was fine.

SUNDAY FARE

Citizens of Houston in Texas who have exotic tastes have to get certain of their supplies in for Sunday eating on the day before unless they want to find their favourite foods unavailable when they go shopping on the Sabbath. An ordinance in place for the last 60 years prevents the sale of a number of mouth-watering specialities such as rye bread, goose livers and Limburger cheese. Why these particular items should have attracted the displeasure of the lawmakers has now long since been forgotten.

PAID IN EGGS

The fees charged by lawyers are a continuing topic of conversation not to mention dispute, but in one part of America they can be settled without argument in eggs, fruit or even vegetables. This holds good in the farming community of Clarendon, Texas, where an old ordinance has been in force for over 150 years that was clearly originally designed to help any hard-up local citizen secure legal aid. The statute says that all lawyers practising in Clarendon must be prepared to accept farm produce in lieu of payment of their fees or else face disbarment.

CHEESED OFF

The Italians take the business of making cheese very seriously and in the northern city of Ferrara it was long ago made an offence for anyone to fall asleep in a factory producing this delicacy. It is also, curiously, against the law for any women of 'ill repute or evil looks' to enter the premises – doubtless those who drew up the law were afraid she might curdle the milk before the manufacturing process began.

WIND OF CHANCE

It is as well not to have hurried through a big meal before going to any church in the American heartland city of Omaha, Nebraska. Good manners have always been insisted upon in this one-time pioneer community and a law on the statute books which is at least a century old declares that it is an offence for anyone to burp or pass wind during a church service. It is actually an offence punishable by a fine – and in the case of an indiscretion by a child, it is the parents who will have to cough up the money.

THE BITTER TASTE OF SCRUMPING

Children all over the world have been unable to resist the temptation of stealing fruit from other people's gardens and orchards. Although in most places when the culprits are caught the worst they can expect is a severe reprimand, in the town of Yuma in Arizona, USA, the authorities have their own unique deterrent in the form of a law passed in the middle of the last century. This decrees that anyone caught stealing oranges, grapefruit, lemons, limes or any other citrus fruit will be punished under the 'Castor Oil' ordinance with 'a good dose of castor oil'.

PIE FACE

One of the oldest laughs in slapstick comedy – the pie in the face – is actually against the law in New Jersey, USA. Although pie-throwing is permitted in theatres and other places of entertainment, it is forbidden in offices and factories. In 1976, a local receptionist actually won $5,000 in an out-of-court settlement after two practical jokers calling themselves Pie in the Eye Inc., who had been hired by some of her friends, walked up to her desk and threw a pie in her face. 'I was not amused,' she protested later, 'I suffered a burning sensation in the eyes and have been forced to quit my job. I have since been under a psychiatrist for nervousness.' Said one of the jokers after being fined $50 for assault, 'It's a shame when it comes to the point that there's not much humour in people. This lady did not have the same attitude as others we have thrown pies at.'

SMASHING DISHES

Chefs and kitchen staff in the American city of Kansas, are still governed by a 100-year-old ordinance that says stacking more than eight plates on top of each other is against the law. Anyone working in a restaurant in Kansas must also never throw any dishes out of a window or they could be in danger of a $50 fine. But it is apparently within the law if the kitchen is on the ground floor – where most are, of course – but not if plate throwing happens to be on the second floor or higher.

OYSTER TRAUMA

A number of American prisoners have taken to suing federal officials for infringement of their civil rights in cases which have been described as 'frivolous, time-consuming or bizarre'. In one, an inmate in New York State prison sued for $1million in compensation because 'warders refused to let me put ice-cream in the prison fridge' which resulted in him 'Suffering deep unhappiness and psychological trauma'. In an even weirder case, a prisoner claimed his constitutional rights were infringed when he developed an ulcer in jail. He sued the authorities for 'failing to provide me with such digestible delicacies as oysters and veal'.

OUT IN THE WASH

Some British prisoners have also followed the lead of their American compatriots behind bars and instituted proceedings against their jailers. One prisoner in Highpoint Prison, Suffolk, recently sued the governor over the quality of his washing powder. He claimed £49 for damage allegedly caused to his clothes by the prison's powder. The inmate, who was serving 21 months for deception and taking part in a riot at a football match, also claimed that the powder was too harsh on his hands.

SPICY DISHES

The authorities in Peru were very concerned about the effects of chilli sauce and other hot spices on the inmates of their prisons. Hence a rule was instituted by the government a few years ago that no dishes with 'aphrodisiac qualities' were to be served in any of the nation's jails. These were felt by the bureaucrats in a gloriously euphemistic statement to be 'inappropriate for men who are forced to live a limited life style'.

LOAD OF TRIPE

Tripe, the dish consisting of part of the stomach of a cow, which has been a popular meal in the north of England for many years, is also subject to a peculiar law in parts of Lancashire. For although it is perfectly legitimate to buy tripe on a Sunday, according to a late nineteenth century ruling 'no vendor may offer for sale on the Sabbath tripe that has been cooked or likewise prepared in any manner'.

SNAKE BITE

In Kansas USA the snake has been a part of folklore and legend for many years. It has also attracted the attention of the makers of strange laws. For according to an ordinance passed in 1804 and never repealed, it is illegal to eat rattlesnake meat on a Sunday in public. This same state also boasts an equally strange ruling that forbids any restaurant from serving gopher pie on the Sabbath.

GOOD NIGHTCAP

It is against the law in France to introduce a sedative of any kind into that traditional prerequisite of a satisfying meal – a bowl of soup. This ancient rule dates back at least 400 years when soup was the mainstay of the diet of many French men and women. It was applied again recently when a Parisian housewife was charged with putting sleeping pills into her husband's soup every night. The reason given for her actions by the mother of seven was 'so he would not want sex with me'.

DRINK SPRINGS ETERNAL

Prohibition in the United States was responsible for the introduction of a draconian law which still exists on the record books of the well-named town of Springs in Pennsylvania. In an effort to control the drinking of errant husbands, the local authorities brought in a ruling that no married man was to be allowed to purchase alcoholic drink without the permission of his wife. And to ensure there was no getting round the law, the wife's consent had to be in writing.

ST PATRICK EVICTED

Officials of the Irish government became so sensitive about the sight of drunken Irishmen cavorting on St Patrick's Day (17 March) that in 1963 they gave serious consideration to changing the date of the national holiday. The tradition of drowning the shamrock – drinking vast amounts of whiskey and Guinness – these officials in Dublin maintained, 'led to irritating comment by foreign journalists'. The proposal was to move the day to September or October. However, no one could agree *why* this might lead to less drinking – and the Irish law that might have been, never was.

RECKLESS ROADS

Drunken drivers pulled over by the police in Massachusetts, USA, might get an even worse hangover after trying to make sense of the wording of one of the statutes that covers this crime in the state: 'Whoever operates an automobile or motorcycle on any public way – laid out under authority of law – recklessly or while under the influence of liquor shall be punished; thereby imposing upon the motorist the duty of finding out at his peril whether certain highways had been laid out recklessly or while under the influence of liquor before driving his car over them.'

JUST THE ONE

A small glass of wine is all that a law in the city of La Paz in Bolivia permits a married woman to take in a public bar or restaurant. This ruling, which has been in force for much of the twentieth century, says that for a female to drink more than one glass is 'morally and sexually lax'. A Bolivian husband may also use the reason that his wife has taken a sip too many as grounds for divorce.

DRY BARS

There is a curious similarity about the laws that govern drinkers in the Canadian province of Saskatchewan and the state of South Carolina on the far side of the continent in the USA. For ordinances in both which have been in place for a century, make it illegal for bartenders to sell – or allow to be drunk – a glass of water.

DRINK IN TIME

A famous sixteenth-century English drinking song, 'The Merry Month of May', which proclaims the joys of cider and the pleasures of romance, was banned from public performance on American TV in 1959. No one has yet got around to lifting this embargo which was imposed because of one word in the lyrics – 'maidenhead'.

SUNK OR DROBER?

The American state of Kentucky is famous for its annual Derby and fine bourbon whisky distillers. It also has on its statute books a fulsome law against drunkenness in public places with perhaps the finest definition of what constitutes being drunk. No one shall be considered drunk in the eyes of the law, it says, 'until he cannot hold onto the ground'.

GIN FOR SIN

Because of an increasing rise in the number of unwanted births in a group of rural communities surrounding Accra in the African country of Ghana, village chiefs there introduced a new system of fines in September 1994. Now any man who gets a girl under 18 pregnant will be fined £30, one sheep and three bottles of gin. The girls, not to be excused their sins, must pay £15.

PINK ELEPHANTS

It is almost literally necessary to claim to see pink elephants in order to get a drink in certain parts of the Indian subcontinent. For there a number of the states have strict laws against the sale of alcohol and in Radesh, for instance, only those with a doctor's certificate can purchase spirits from the few stores which are licensed to sell such items. This certificate must confirm that 'the bearer is a chronic alcoholic and is unable to survive without a regular intake of alcohol'.

HIP FLASKS

The drinking man who likes to carry a hip flask around with him is in real danger of breaking the law in the town of Greenwood in South Carolina, USA. Because here a local ordinance was introduced in the early years of the nineteenth century that no man should be allowed to have hip pockets on his trousers. The local authorities – teetotallers, no doubt – had decided that such pockets would only be used for carrying bottles of booze.

COLD COMFORT

Life in the vast, hostile territory of Quebec in northern Canada has never been easy for any of its inhabitants – least of all the Indians. A law introduced ostensibly to curb drinking among these people still makes it difficult for them to travel by motor transport during the snowbound winter months. For this says it is illegal for anyone to sell Indians ... anti-freeze.

FUNERAL RATIONS

According to an old statute book in Boston, Massachusetts, it is illegal for citizens to serve alcoholic drinks to mourners at a funeral service. The mean-spirited lawmakers who drew up the original law also said that there should be just one cup of tea or coffee per person – and no person was to be allowed more than three sandwiches. There was also no chance whatsoever of having your cake and eating it.

3

CORPORATE BODIES

Quaint Laws Of the Professions

London taxi drivers are probably subjected to more curious old laws than any other profession. The men who ply their trade in cabs through the busy streets of the capital city are answerable to no fewer than 37 Hackney Carriage Acts – most of which date from the last century, although there are a few which go back as far as the reign of Queen Anne in the first decade of the eighteenth century. None of these rules has ever been repealed – and if enforced today would undoubtedly result in thousands of prosecutions on every day of the week ...

Take, for example the simple business of hailing a cab. According to the letter of these old laws, it is illegal to shout out 'Taxi!' while a cab is in motion. Passengers wanting to make a journey should actually go to a taxi rank or – to use the phrase in the old statute – 'place appointed'. From the days of horse-drawn cabs, another law insists that cabbies should always carry a nose-bag on the side of their vehicle, 'in order to have sufficient foodstuffs for the horse'. No London cabbie is allowed to carry a passenger suffering from any 'notifiable disease such as smallpox or the plague'. He is, in fact, empowered to carry out an examination of any fare he suspects might have a contagious disease – because if he is caught by a custodian of the law with an ill passenger on board he is the one who will be prosecuted.

Another law threatens a hefty fine for the cabbie who makes 'insulting gestures', while two more govern his speed. Any driver who goes too slowly or holds up traffic can be prosecuted for 'loitering', and it is equally an offence within the city limits to drive 'too furiously'. But perhaps the strangest of all is the law which stems from the fact it is illegal for a cabbie to leave his vehicle on a public thoroughfare. For this reason he is permitted when nature calls to relieve himself at the rear of his vehicle 'in a seemly fashion'.

41

THIEVES' CHARTER

Another English rule jokingly called the 'Thieves Charter' which has been on the statute books for even longer – over 800 years, in fact – has actually just been repealed. Officially termed the 'Market Overt Rules', these state that any items bought from a market stallholder 'between sunrise and sunset' become the legal property of the buyer – even if it turns out they have been stolen. As a result, many markets have for centuries been exempt from the usual laws governing stolen property; while the original owner, who may well have lost the property in a burglary, had no legal redress. Introduced in 1189, the laws were regarded by many as a valuable form of 'consumer protection' – that is until the government stepped in and abolished them by Act of Parliament in January 1995. The biggest of these London markets – Bermondsey Antiques Market – still attracts over 500 stallholders and until that fateful January was famous for being the place to offload goods which 'fell off the back of a lorry'.

THE DEVIL'S WORK

Transylvania in Romania is famous, of course, as the home of Count Dracula, the vampire the world loves to hate. Although this bloodsucker was actually a figment of the imagination of author Bram Stoker, this is a country where superstition still plays a part in daily life. In the town of Sibiu, for instance, which nestles at the foot of the Transylvanian Alps, the practice of hypnotism is regarded as 'the work of the devil' and a number of the professions are specifically banned by law from using it on customers. Among these are doctors, dentists and even the proprietors of bars, cafés and restaurants.

DAMP COPPER

The policemen and women in the rural town of Omaha in

Nebraska, USA, are understandably not keen on rain – because a local statute does not allow them to carry umbrellas. The same rule book also forbids the men from being seen walking around with their hands in their pockets. *That* can earn them a stiff rap over the knuckles in the form of disciplinary action or a fine.

NO-FLY ZONE

Health officials in the teeming Chinese city of Guangzhou have recently instituted a new campaign to try and cut down the high instances of disease in some of the poorer quarters. Among the rules that have been added to the statute books for the local health inspectors to act upon is one that threatens, 'a fine of £150 for each fly found on a resident's premises'.

DEATH DUTIES

The tax inspectors in Minnesota, the rural American state near the Great Lakes which is renowned for its farming co-operatives, have not made the lives of their taxpayers any easier by producing one of the most comprehensive tax forms in the USA. Even after completing the various sections from name and address to an estimation of fiscal liability, the Minnesotan is still not quite finished. There is one last section that needs to be completed which reads: 'Date of death'.

TORN IT

Although German law allows its civil servants to claim expenses incurred while carrying out their duties, the rules do not cover damage to clothing. This resulted in a court case when a civil servant in Bonn tore his trousers on a nail in the Ministry of Defence building and put in a £20 claim for repairs. When he was offered £2 in compensation, the man began litigation which lasted for five years. The recent judgement decided the £2 offered had been 'adequate'. In the interim, the hapless civil servant had run up legal costs of over £500.

INVISIBLE MEN

The Swiss authorities who for generations have prided themselves on preserving the anonymity of those who use their banks – foreigners especially – have recently done an about-turn over people seeking asylum in the country. A new law has been passed which increases the powers of the police to jail foreigners who fail to identify themselves satisfactorily. The authorities are also free now – the ruling states – to search the homes of these 'non-existent aliens'.

STOCK IN THE OLDEST TRADE

Probably the most irregular shares ever offered to potential investors on New York's Wall Street were in a German brothel. These were proffered by a consortium of German businessmen in the winter of 1973. The offer of the house of ill-fame caught the eye of the Securities and Exchange Commission – the US Government Agency which supervises dealings on the stock exchange – who promptly filed a lawsuit in January 1974. The reason for the complaint was hilarious: 'That the vendors had failed to justify their claim that shareholders would double their money within ten months'.

INTO THE UNKNOWN

The Attorney-General of New York State is each year faced with keeping a watchful eye on illegal charities which attempt to beat the law and play on the gullibility of the general public. Amongst the most profitable of these scams in recent years which the

Attorney finally caught up with and closed down was one glorying in the title of 'The Fund for the Widow of the Unknown Soldier'.

BITING NUN

The Canadian authorities have also had trouble with people collecting for charity – but no law officer had encountered anyone quite like the nun one policeman found trying to collect money on the streets of Montreal in 1985. When he tried to arrest her for soliciting donations without a permit, the nun turned round and bit him. Only later at the station did the officer discover the name of her order – The Apostles of Infinite Love.

THE LAW OUTLAWED

Though the attitude of members of the public towards lawyers is often very ambivalent, in only one country of the world are they actually banned. This is the case in Andorra, the tiny country tucked away in the Pyrenees mountains, sandwiched between France and Spain. Here a rule was introduced in 1864 which stated unequivocally, if amusingly: 'The appearance in our courts of the learned gentlemen of the law, who can make black appear white and white appear black, is forbidden.' (In actual fact, the country does today allow *one* lawyer to practise in Andorra la Vella – but he only conveys property and drafts wills – he never goes to court.)

GUNNED DOWN

An attempt to use the law against the surgeon who had saved a gangster's life made legal history when it came to court in the American city of Pittsburgh, Pennsylvania, in 1960. Gunman Frank Gaito had been shot by police during an armed raid and it had taken all the skill of the surgeon who operated on him to remove a bullet lodged close to his heart. This missile was then used in evidence to convict Gaito. Once in prison, however, the gunman attempted to sue the surgeon for £150,000 for 'illegal search and seizure'.

TOOTHLESS LAW

Practising as a dentist has never been without its problems. But there is an old statute that has never been repealed in the small American community of South Foster, Rhode Island, which would make anyone think twice about taking up the profession. No doubt it was drawn up in rougher and readier times: but it effectively allows anyone who has had a tooth wrongly pulled by a dentist to insist he himself has the same thing done by way of restitution. And the man to perform the 'operation' should be the local blacksmith.

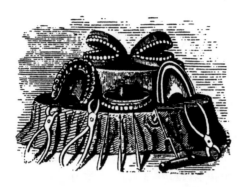

THE LAUGHING CLERGYMAN

The clergyman with a sense of humour can have a hard time if he wants to introduce some light relief into his Sunday sermons in prim little Nicholas County in West Virginia, USA. For here, 200 years ago, the lawmakers decreed that no jokes or humorous stories were to be told from the pulpit as they 'distract the minds of the congregation from the seriousness of worship'. Any clergyman who does dare to flout this ban and introduce a bit of levity into his message can actually be barred from his church by the local police. He may also be fined a month's salary, but only as long as he agrees not to repeat the 'offence'.

THE LAW OF THE LAY

Professors of the University of Paris are still governed by a thirteenth-century law which makes it illegal for them to seduce female students. In 1215, after a number of women at the university had allegedly been made pregnant by their tutors, a rule was introduced by the authorities which has never been rescinded. This expressly forbids intercourse between staff and students within the university buildings as it is 'an exaggeration against good manners and decency, a scoffing against God and the Church, a worldly vanity, and' – saving the best for last – 'a mad presumption'.

SHINING EXAMPLE

Over the years, many British MPs have turned up at the Houses of Parliament in all manner of curious dress. There is, however, one item of apparel that is specifically banned by a law that was passed as long ago as 1313 during the reign of Edward II and which has never been repealed. This forbids any member from entering the House wearing a suit of armour.

DRESSING DOWN

The profession of window dresser in the city of Liverpool has one drawback if a law passed by the local authorities between the two world wars is ever put into effect. For in this city famous as the birthplace of The Beatles – all of whom would surely have found the ruling hilarious – it is unlawful to 'dress or undress a female mannequin in the window of any store or shop where children might observe the unclothed model'. The same statute also forbids any child from 'peering up the dress of a mannequin' – though it is the parents who are likely to suffer by being taken to court and fined.

THE TIGHT OF FASHION

Dressmakers in Nalagonda, near Hyderabad in India, are still likely to fall foul of the law if they send a female customer out into the streets with a dress that it is too figure revealing. A local authority ruling, which was brought into force during the early years of the British Raj, forbids any female from wearing 'an item of clothing which clings to her person and thereby excites attention' when she is out in public.

A STAY IN TIME

The manufacturers of women's underwear – corset makers in particular – would do well to consult the old statute books in the famous American coastal port of Norfolk, Virginia, if they are looking for extra business. For here, where the US Navy maintains the headquarters of its Atlantic Fleet, women are required by a local law to always be wearing corsets when they appear in public. It is in dance halls and night clubs that the ordinance is at its most restrictive, because no woman is permitted to remove her corset before she goes on to the dance floor or adjust it while she is tripping the light fantastic. Curiously, it is not the females who commit this 'wanton activity' – as the original lawmakers defined it – who are likely to be fined, but the owner of the premises, who can even be shut down by the police for permitting such a terrible breach of the law.

REDUCED MEASUREMENTS

Dressmakers in Salzburg, Austria were for years able to offer women with small bosoms a special discount whenever they bought clothes. Because of an old law that lumped the measurements of men and women together in a ruling first issued in the eighteenth century by the local authorities, any female with breasts of less than 32 inches was entitled to pay ten per cent less than her more well endowed sisters.

AWFUL HATS

Milliners in Milan, Italy – the town which gave its name to the sale of fancy goods, especially headgear – have long had to be careful about an ancient ruling which prohibits them from manufacturing any hats that might 'cause offence to nervous people, children and animals'.

MAKE-UP BAN

Beauticians would have a hard time making a living in the town of Morrisville in Pennsylvania, USA, if an old law from the last century was strictly applied. Because this says that unless a women is prepared to buy a special permit from the local authorities she may not wear any kind of 'make-up, lipstick or eyeshadow'.

MOTHER CHRISTMAS

There is certainly one place where the rise of feminism has had no effect on an old law about impersonating Father Christmas during the festive season. Throughout the American state of Minnesota a nineteenth-century piece of legislation threatens a fine of $50 or 30 days in jail for any woman who 'dresses up and appears in public in the guise of Father Christmas'.

HOLE IN THE CASE

A doughnut vendor who continued selling his goods in the historic Market Cross in Chichester, Sussex, despite repeated prosecutions, believed a 500-year-old edict by the Bishop of Chichester gave him the right to defy the might of modern municipal regulations. For when the bishop had sold the cross in 1501 he had specified that 'peasants should be free to sell goods there without let or hindrance from the mayor or established traders'. The doughnut seller had discovered the edict in a local library but, when the matter went to the Court of Appeal in December 1994, the lords justices ruled that it had actually been superseded by a ban on street traders passed in 1807. 'I am willing to accept the interpretation,' the vendor said with a wry smile later, 'but I did think for a while I'd found a hole in the law.'

FLAMING PROBLEMS

Firemen in the magnificent old port of St Louis, on the west bank of the Mississippi, have one ever-present problem on their hands whenever they are fire-fighting, thanks to an old statute passed in the prim and proper years of the nineteenth century. For this expressly forbids them from rescuing any female who is not fully dressed. Unless she can quickly slip into something more substantial and less revealing, no woman in 'a nightgown, chemise or bath robe' may legally be aided by a fireman. But there's obviously been many a slip between rescue and this law.

EXPLOSIVE REMEDY

Chemists in the American state of Utah were renowned during the nineteenth century for some of the alarming potions and lotions they sold to customers. Then the lawmakers moved in to protect the unsuspecting with the introduction of a number of curious laws. Perhaps the strangest is to be found in the tiny little community of Troutcreek where one former remedy for headaches is now prohibited. It consisted of a mixture of spirits and gunpowder.

LICENSED TO PERM

Hairdressers in the American state of Nebraska have had their livelihood protected for a number of years by a strange old piece of legislation that prevents any woman giving another member of her sex a permanent wave unless she has a state licence. A similar ruling also applies in a number of other places in America where certain ancient laws even threaten any woman who does her own hair with prosecution if she isn't properly registered.

SHAVE A LEG

Barbers in the town of Carrizozo, New Mexico are often kept busier by women customers than men – thanks to an old law which is apparently still widely observed. This rule, which was introduced in the middle of the nineteenth century, declared that an unshaven women was 'an affront to God and man' and she should not be allowed to appear in public displaying any facial or leg hair. If she did, she ran the risk of being publicly shaved as an example to others.

HAIR BREATH

Members of the hairdressing profession in the central US city of Nebraska cannot hope for the winds of the Great Plains to blow their troubles away if they fall foul of one old law which is still on the statute books. This was first passed in 1910 and threatens a barber with a fine and possible closure of his business for repeated offences. The ordinance states: 'It shall be illegal for any barber to eat onions between 7 am and 7 pm.'

CHARMING WAYS

A peculiar law in the African country of Zimbabwe permits citizens to sell shrunken heads, but forbids them from selling any human organs. This law was recently seen in action in the nation's capital, Harare, in January 1995, when a man was fined £30 for offering sun-dried human hearts which he had allegedly stolen from a hospital. The culprit alleged he was selling the items as magical charms.

THE DEMON BARBER

Sweeney Todd, the infamous 'Demon Barber of Fleet Street', who is alleged to have murdered hundreds of his customers and then passed their corpses to his partner-in-crime next door to dispose of in pork pies, is also remembered for his greeting to customers to 'polish them off' as they sat down in his chair. With the growth of the legend about Todd, many towns took legal steps to ensure the safety of customers in their local barber shops. These even spread across the Channel to France, where the lawmakers in Amiens made it an offence punishable by a stiff fine for any hairdresser to threaten – even in jest – to 'cut off the nose or ears of a customer'. It is also against the law in the town to allow anyone to fall asleep in a barber's chair.

BURNED TO A CINDER

For over 600 years a dire threat has hung over the head of English butchers. For, in the fourteenth century, a law was instituted that ruled that any member of the profession found guilty of selling bad meat was to be put in the pillory for a day. The statute, which has never been repealed, added that the hapless butcher was to have his rotten meat burnt beneath him while he sat there.

BOOK AT BEDTIME

Librarians in Widnes, Lancashire, now have the law on their side to prevent people from falling asleep in the reading rooms or resting on the floors – both offences are subject to fines of £5 under new by-laws. However, library officials have been quick to point out that no such penalties would be imposed on those who dropped off 'by accident' or any short-sighted reader 'who had to lie down to read titles on the bottom shelves'.

LOO ROLLS

There are numerous English laws that govern the provision of toilet facilities for workers in factories and offices. Some of the oldest date from the early years of the Victorian era, but a number of the more recent additions have thrown up unexpected problems. A Sussex furniture factory owner learned all about one in 1993 when he was charged with failing to provide proper toilets for his female staff. Yet the man also revealed a bit of old-fashioned chivalry when appearing in court and informing the magistrate, 'There is only one toilet facility in the factory and that is used by the men. As my secretary declines to use this facility, I drive her to the toilet in Littlehampton Railway Station whenever it is necessary.'

DICTATING THE RULES

Any secretary who has ever had a moment's anxiety about the familiarity of her boss could do worse than move to Pasadena, the California resort city famous for its annual Tournament of the Roses and star-gazing observatories at Mount Palomar and Mount Wilson. Because here a local ordinance makes it illegal for a secretary ever to be alone in the office with her boss.

SLEEPING NAKED

Hotel owners in Salem, Massachusetts, the American city forever associated with the notorious witch trials of 1692, are bound by a curious local ordinance that no guests may be allowed to sleep naked in their rooms. The hoteliers are breaking the law if any man or woman – even a married couple – stay overnight and do not go to bed in some form of garment. The law insists that before they go to their rooms each and every guest must be supplied with 'a freshly laundered and ironed night shirt'.

A SPIT IN TIME

Storekeepers and hotel owners in El Paso, the famous frontier city on the border between America and Mexico which has replaced a violent past with a guided missiles experiment station, are now governed by a special law about human missiles. This is explained in Section 338 of the El Paso statutes under the heading, 'Hotels and All Public Places of Resort', which reads: 'In and at all public places of resort and amusement, such as hotels or halls of assembly, or stores or markets or banking rooms or railroad depots or waiting stations or saloons, shall be required at the expense of the owners or persons in charge of same, or under whose control or care the same are, to be provided with spittoons of a kind and number to efficiently contain expectorations into them.'

DUSTY ROOMS

The managers of hotels throughout the large American city of Pittsburgh in Pennsylvania have to take great care that their chambermaids don't fall foul of an old piece of legislation that is still on the rule books almost 200 years after it was instituted. This forbids the hiding of dust under the carpets in any room, although it is no offence to brush it into a cupboard.

A STICKY MATTER

All managers of cinemas and theatres know the problem with patrons who will insist on sticking chewing gum under their seats or in other parts of the auditorium, thereby making cleaning difficult. This annoying habit so exercised the lawmakers of New York that they recently passed a law requiring all theatre owners to 'scrape up gum from beneath seats at least once every month'. Sticky-finger undercover agents are to inspect premises without warning, a report added.

OUT OF TUNE

The beautiful city of Strasbourg beside the River Rhine on the French-German border has a fine reputation for its music, but still harbours one peculiar law that has apparently never been repealed. This applies to pianists – but one-armed pianists in particular. Because according to this ruling such men may only play in public 'as long as no admission fee is charged for the performance'.

BUILDING FOR THE FUTURE

Irish property owners, faced with a new Landlord and Tenant Act in 1927, were intrigued shortly afterwards by news that a treatise on the law explaining in simpler terms some of its more obscure points was due for publication in 1931 in the *Irish Law Times*. The year duly arrived and yet nothing appeared in the journal. In fact, another decade was to pass before the *Times* published the article, prefacing it with an apology, 'that we had not an earlier opportunity to draw our readers' attention to this Act'.

MILK OF KINDNESS

Farmers in the old pioneer state of Virginia – the first of the Thirteen Colonies to be founded in America – need to watch their language or else they can be subjected to some rather unusual punishments, according to a statute that was introduced in 1624. No man must show disrespect to a woman or else risk being forced to 'stand in front of a church wrapped in a white sheet for three Sundays running'. The worst crime of all is to accuse a lady of being a slut – for the offender will be punished by being 'drenched in one pottle [half a gallon] of milk per day at the cow pen until the last day of September'.

PRIVATE MAIL

Postmen in the American state of Montana face a delicate task when handing over a husband's mail to his wife. For a nineteenth-century ruling still decrees that it is an offence punishable by law for a wife to open any letter addressed to her spouse. Even a plea in a court of law that a woman has good reason to read any correspondence which she suspects may show her husband is being unfaithful is still inadmissible in Montana. This law is regarded as yet another example of an ordinance passed by men – because there is nothing in it to prevent a man opening anything addressed to his wife.

CLOTHES LINES

The job of being a laundryman has special problems in the aptly named little American community of Nappanee, Indiana. Although the town's lawmakers first introduced the unusual local rules about the hanging of washing on lines for the benefit of householders, a rider to the law was added later to include laundry businesses. One of the dozen rules governing washing states that 'no housewife is to hang clothing on a line of more than 50 inches length'; while another insists that no women's underwear should be hung on any line outside a building. Laundry workers have also been told that it is against the law to dampen clothes they are ironing 'with any liquid, such as water, alcohol or spirits, that has been sprayed from the mouth'.

DON'T-DO-IT-YOURSELF

Carpenters who happen to live in the town of Schenectady in New York State are actually prevented from following their profession on Sundays by an old law that has been in force for almost a century. For reasons that are not quite clear, a rule was brought into force in the town that 'no nail holes may be bored and filled' on the Sabbath. A theory has been advanced that this may somehow relate to the crucifixion of Jesus Christ, but notwithstanding this the law also includes any householder or do-it-yourself enthusiast in Schenectady who also might want to carry out repairs. At another small town not far away, Passaic in New Jersey, it is against the law to carry out any painting of a house or building on Sundays.

OUT ON A LIMB

A Canadian sculptor was charged with conduct likely to cause a breach of the peace in Brighton, Sussex, in January 1986. His grisly appeal was one the magistrates had never heard before and the police found difficult to categorize. The artist had asked for 'human limbs that I can use in my sculptures'.

THE LAST ACT

The 1951 United Kingdom Finance Act contains this delightful piece of phraseology on its last page under Section 36 (10): 'And a body corporate shall not be deemed for the purpose of this section to cease to be resident in the United Kingdom by reason only that it ceases to exist.'

4

LAW AND

DISORDER

Curious Legalities Of Public Behaviour

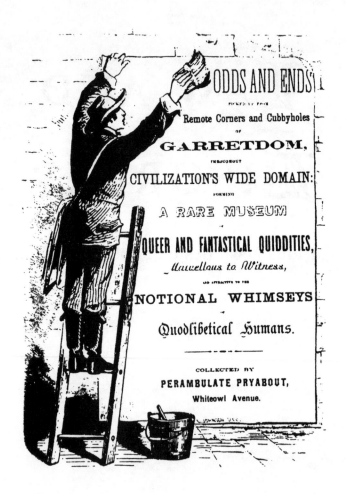

ODDS AND ENDS

PICKED UP FROM

Remote Corners and Cubbyholes

OF

GARRETDOM,

THROUGHOUT

CIVILIZATION'S WIDE DOMAIN:

FORMING

A RARE MUSEUM

OF

QUEER AND FANTASTICAL QUIDDITIES,

Marvellous to Witness,

AND ATTRACTIVE TO THE

NOTIONAL WHIMSEYS

OF

Quodlibetical Humans.

COLLECTED BY

PERAMBULATE PRYABOUT,

Whiteowl Avenue.

The notorious 'bill poster', who is always being threatened with prosecution on walls and derelict shop fronts throughout the British Isles, has probably never been involved in an odder case of illegal fly posting than the events in 1987. These featured a policeman with a sense of humour and a poster depicting the prime minister dressed in fishnet stockings, suspenders and wielding a leather whip. Printed on the offending montage were the words, 'On your knees to Madame M. You must make up your mind – do you want to work with madame or not?'

The poster, which was on the point of being put up in Kensington High Street three days before a general election, resulted in the artist appearing before magistrates for committing an offence under the laws against fly posting as well as the new Public Order Act, 1986. Section 51 b of this Act now makes it an offence punishable with a fine of up to £400 if a person 'displays as writing, sign or other visible representation which is threatening, abusive or insulting within the hearing or sight of a person likely to be caused harassment, alarm or distress.'

According to the prosecution, a policeman on patrol had seen the poster going up on a wall and had arrested the artist before he could complete the job. When the PC was asked in court what his reaction to the poster had been, he said it was 'funny ... I wouldn't say very funny'. In reply, the defence counsel argued that the prosecution had failed to produce any victim who had been 'harassed, alarmed or distressed' – and in any event the almost-laughing policeman had found the poster funny.

Perhaps not surprisingly, the magistrates ruled there was no charge to answer – and the case became yet another quirk among a number of strange laws governing public behaviour ...

GO-GO TOPLESS

A loophole in the law put the authorities in the city of Birmingham into an embarrassing situation when they introduced a statute in the 1960s about the appearance of go-go dancers in local clubs. The ruling was unequivocal: anyone who performed go-go dancing on a stage in public must wear a bra. Red-faced committee members soon learned that the wording they had agonized over indicated that *men* were just as liable under the restriction as women. A rapid rethink took place after a number of complaints had been lodged, and a subsequent amendment was issued in which the Birmingham authority stated they 'recognized there were differences between men and women' and that, in future, 'no male go-go dancer was hereafter required to wear a brassière'.

STREETWISE STYLE

At least two American cities are very hard on unsuitably dressed citizens. In Denver, the state capital of Colorado, famous for its metropolitan outlook, there is still a law that makes wearing 'unattractive clothing' punishable by a fine. In Carmel, New York, an old ordinance is even more specific: there no male citizen may be seen in the streets wearing wearing 'a jacket and trouser pants that are not matched' unless he wants to end up in court and collect a fine of $50.

ELBOWED OUT

The fashion-conscious woman in the famous old city of Jerusalem now has a clothing hazard to avoid unless she wants to risk the break-up of her marriage if she happens to be wed to a prudish husband. Because, according to a new statute issued in August 1994 by Rabbi Moshe Bitan, 'women who expose their elbows, even in sweltering heat, give their husbands sufficient reason for a divorce.'

BELLY DANCING

After centuries of uninterrupted performance, the time-honoured Egyptian belly dance has finally attracted the attention of the country's lawmakers. Not that the dancers have been asked to change their costumes or even the style of dancing. It is the belly button itself that has come under scrutiny. For, following complaints in 1986 that naked belly buttons constituted an affront to Muslim women, a rule was introduced that all dancers appearing in public places must now 'cover the offending part with a strip of gauze'.

PRIVATE PARTS

Allegedly indecent behaviour is also a subject of numerous laws in the Italian city of Venice. One deals specifically with nudity and brought Giorgio Spiler, who described himself as a 'behavioural artist', before a court in November 1982. Giorgio was charged under the statute following his arrest in the Piazza San Marco where he had been found dressed as a six-foot-high penis. When no codicil could be found to cover this specific case of indecent behaviour, the artist was acquitted. Later, while the statutes were being reviewed, Giorgio said he found the whole case ridiculous. 'Last year I dressed up as a vagina and there was no trouble,' he said.

TAX TIPS

An American striptease dancer recently used her biggest assets as an argument to beat the tax authorities in Indiana in April 1994. The stripper, who gave her name as Chesty Love, claimed the cost of enlarging her breasts from 36B to a huge 56FF was tax deductible. After hearing the case, the judge agreed to her being allowed relief on the $1,500 operation because it was 'part of her job'.

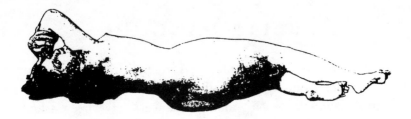

PROMISES, PROMISES

Displays of 'lewd behaviour' are forbidden in the town of Fiox in France, but this did not prevent a 22-year-old woman from stripping at a local dance in December 1982. She was fined 2,000 francs for taking off all her clothes after the band leader had promised to reward her with a free television set and tape recorder. He did not keep his promise.

CROSS DRESSING

Though cross dressing has become an almost accepted fact of life in many countries, this is not the case in the Irish town of Mullingar, Westmeath, which sits beside the Royal Canal on its meandering journey to Dublin. For here a law has been in place for over 200 years that threatens a stiff fine and the possibility of a period in jail for any man or woman 'who appears in public dressed with the intent to disguise his or her sex as that of the opposite sex'.

TOP FREE

In July 1994, a group of women in New York began riding on the city's subways naked from the waist up. Calling themselves Top Free, they claimed to be testing a curious law passed a couple of years earlier when the Court of Appeal ruled that an anti-nudity law decreeing that only men could bare their chests in public was wrong because it discriminated against women. Top Free insisted that 'female breasts were no different from male ones' – indeed! – and if enough were seen of them, 'they would no longer be considered erotic'. Unfortunately, a more recent report says, one of the most dedicated Top Free campaigners now has to 'carry a water pistol to deter persistent starers'.

BELIEVE IT OR NOT

Kevin Winterbottom was the name of a man charged with insulting behaviour when he ran naked from the waist down on to the pitch at Twickenham during the England v Scotland rugby match in March 1983 ... A defendant who appeared in another English court in July 1986 was called Nauti Raskal... while a few days after this a man with an even more apt name was fined £200 by the Torquay magistrates for swearing at the police. He was Nicholas Forletta.

STREAK OF BAD LUCK

It certainly does not pay to get drunk and do a streak anywhere in the African country of Kenya. Especially not if the streaker is a foreign visitor, for a ruling that recently went onto the country's statute books has a very summary way of dealing with such law breakers. 'Any foreign national who flouts this rule will be immediately arrested,' a spokesmen announced when details of the law were made public, 'escorted directly to the airport in the nude and there put aboard the first available aircraft to his country of origin. All of his clothes will be confiscated by the Kenyan authorities.'

UGLY LAW

An ordinance which today seems heartless and unfeeling is still on the statute books in the American city of Chicago, Illinois, where it is unaffectionately known as the 'Ugly Law'. The wording of this particular ruling explains everything: 'No person who is diseased, maimed, mutilated or in any way deformed so as to be an unsightly or disgusting object, or an improper person to be allowed in or on the public ways or other public places in this city, shall not therein or thereon expose himself to public view, under a penalty of not less than one dollar nor more than $50 for each offense.'

DON'T MENTION SEX

'Felonious sexual penetration' was the charge brought against a 42-year-old man in Cincinnati, USA, by a 29-year-old woman who said in court that she fainted at the mention of the word 'sex'. The man had apparently whispered the word in her ear in the lobby of her apartment building, whereupon she passed out. During the preliminary hearings, the woman fainted six times at the mention of the troublesome word and in the end it was substituted with 'nookie' for the trial proper. The hapless man pleaded not guilty 'by reason of insanity'.

STRIPTEASE DEATHS

When a number of citizens of the small town of Kiryat Malachi in southern Israel broke a local law by attending a striptease show they could never have guessed the outcome. For within a week six people had died from various causes. The local rabbi blamed the show for the deaths and ordered an immediate fast and sacrifice to atone. The striptease was the first to have been held in the town's thirty-year history.

BAD LANGUAGE

The authorities in Jacksonville, Illinois, have very firm views about noise in their community. Indeed an ordinance laid down in 1884 by the city elders of this community not far from the great American fun-loving city of St Louis is still in force. 'No person,' it states, 'shall halloo, shout, bawl, scream, use profane language, dance, sing, whoop, quarrel, or make any unusual noise or sound in any house in such manner as to disturb the peace and quiet of the neighborhood.'

THE SILENT ISLAND

Hawaii, famous for its hospitality and beautiful girls, also has a strict control on noise levels. Island laws prevent any 'loud noises' being made on Sundays, while laughing in the streets after 10 pm can earn the culprit a $50 fine. Singing, however, is encouraged, and one time-honoured rule permits Hawaiian men to serenade their wives and girlfriends all through the night if they wish – as long as they do it on a beach.

EROTIC FUNERALS

Despite the fact that Taiwan has strict laws against public nudity, a craze has developed in the Asian country for striptease performances at funerals. 'Rich people who like to show off their wealth are organizing these displays and turning funerals into farces,' an official statement deplored. Yet the country's lawmakers are, apparently, loath to ban these 'erotic burials' because they believe they may well qualify as 'legitimate displays of ancestor worship'.

LINES OF INTIMACY

Despite its hardy past as a place where a living had to be grubbed from the soil in farming or by lumbering, the state of Minnesota in the north of America still has a curiously prim law on its statute books. It concerns washing hung out to dry – for, according to a ruling introduced just after Minnesota became the thirty-second state of the Union in 1858, it is illegal for 'male and female underwear to hang on the same washing line'.

ARDOUR COOLED

In the Egyptian capital of Cairo it is against the law to 'offend a woman's modesty in a public place'. In March 1995, an accountant found himself jailed for a month on these grounds for accosting a woman out walking with her fiancé in a Cairo street. 'Oh, you are so beautiful and delicious,' the man of figures was alleged to have said. 'You are much better looking than him.'

SMELL OF TROUBLE

The American state of Indiana, which has a reputation for battling for its rights ever since farmers fought against the rising tide of industry in the closing years of the last century, is still pretty hot on those who offend today. For in this part of the USA where food processing has become big business, there is still a ban which prevents any citizen riding on a bus 'within four hours of eating garlic'.

ROLL OUT THE BARREL

That famous London expression, 'Roll Out the Barrel' actually describes an illegal act. Because, according to the Metropolitan Police Act of 1839, it is an offence punishable with a £20 fine to 'roll, cleanse, hoop, fire, wash or scald' a cask or tub on any footway in the Greater London area. The only exception is if the barrel is being loaded or unloaded from a cart. The same also applies to hoops and wheels.

GESTURE OF OFFENCE

In a number of countries around the world it is against the law to make offensive gestures at civic dignitaries. In the city of Columbus, in Montana, USA, for instance, any person who does not raise his hat to the mayor as he passes in the street is likely to be charged with a misdemeanour. The same is also true here in Newcastle, where a man was recently brought before magistrates for 'making a two-fingered gesture' at the mayor. The defendant was acquitted when he claimed that he had 'mistaken the mayor for a judge'.

UP IN SMOKE

The efforts of the authorities in New York City to clean up the environment could perhaps take another leap forward if anyone chose to enforce an old ordinance which has never been repealed. For this ruling, which was introduced in 1789 when New York was briefly the nation's first capital under the Constitution, made it illegal 'for members of the female sex to smoke in public places'.

RUDE AWAKENING

Sunbathing in the nude has become increasingly commonplace in recent years on the world's beaches. But there are still certain stretches of golden sand where curious laws persist. Take Palermo in Sicily, for example, where any young girl is free to take off all her clothes, but the man who wants to snooze in the sun must keep his swimming trunks on. A fine of £5 awaits the man who disobeys because, says the local rule in a wonderfully euphemistic sentence, 'the male anatomical conformation can become obscene, *even unconsciously*'. (My italics.)

TIGHTROPE WALKING

The town of Winchester in Massachusetts, USA, had a reputation for many years for the extreme strictness of a number of its laws governing what could and could not be done on Sundays – laws that had been introduced to keep the day holy. Among the 'immoralities' banned were cursing (with an added fine if the words 'God' or 'Jesus' were part of the profanity), the selling of toys and the practice of tightrope walking. There was, though, a quite hilarious proviso to this last activity. 'A young lady may not be employed to dance on a tightrope on Sunday,' the appropriate law stated, 'unless she is in a church.'

FUNNY FACE

Despite its association with one of the most amusing cartoon characters, Garfield County in Montana, USA, has a special local law forbidding comic sketches on window shades. This ban on funny faces was introduced early in the nineteenth century when a particularly bitter local election campaign produced a spate of offensive caricatures of the rival candidates being hung up in the windows of shops and houses. Supporters of the opponents then took to smashing these windows, causing considerable damage. After the campaign was over, the winning candidate – surprise, surprise – convinced the local authorities that the best way of preventing further outbreaks of this kind would be to introduce an ordinance that would make it an offence punishable with a $200 fine to 'draw cartoons or funny faces on shades'. In order not to appear too draconian, however, the lawmakers agreed that it should only be an offence if the pictures could be seen when the shades were *down*.

SUCKED IN

The humble vacuum cleaner, invented by the Scotsman Hubert Cecil Booth in 1901, ran foul of the law not many years later when salesmen began taking the machines around the countryside to sell to British housewives. In several districts, it was declared illegal for these men to try to encourage a woman to buy one anywhere in public on a Sunday. The law was actually introduced in deference to the much older rules governing commerce on the Sabbath – though apparently the ban did not prevent the clever salesman from trying to make a sale as long as he could talk his way into a potential customer's house before making his pitch.

CIGARETTE BAN

Curiously, one of the earliest bans against smoking in public places was introduced in the American Wild West in the old frontier town of Fargo, North Dakota. Here, over a century and a half ago, the local lawmakers laid down the rule that no man was allowed to smoke a cigarette in the presence of a woman. There appears to have been some pretty strong objections to this law from the male population while it was being passed, because a loophole was provided for the town's smokers by specifically avoiding any mention of cigars or pipes.

PARKING HORROR

The Bois de Boulogne in Paris has recently become something of a nightmare for visitors following the introduction of some tough, if not a little strange, new by-laws covering the capital's famous park. People who are now banned include 'Persons who are drunk or dirty, beggars, musicians, singers and any other persons carrying a burden likely to inconvenience others. Sports attire is tolerated only for persons engaged in exercises.' Nor does the legislation end there. For the law says that written permission from the Prefect of Police is required to do any of the following things: clean cars, beat carpets, light fires, use catapults or 'sing in chorus'.

CRIMINAL'S LAW

Even American criminals are now liable under their own anti-crime law which they must observe if they happen to follow their profession in Texas, USA. The Lone Star State three years ago introduced a legal document that requires a criminal 'to give his or her intended victim 24 hours notice prior to the commission of the crime, either orally or in writing'. The legislators were not quite finished there, either. For apart from being asked to inform their victims precisely what type of crime they are going to be subjected to, lawbreakers have to indicate the time and place at which it will be committed. All confessions gratefully received.

FAWKING OUT

The story of Guy Fawkes who was arrested in the cellars beneath the Houses of Parliament and executed for his part in the ill-fated Gunpowder Plot to blow up the king, is familiar to every child. The events of the night of 5 November 1605 have, of course, been marked for many years since by bonfires and the burning of guys, as well as inspiring two curious laws. The first, which remained in force until 1859, made it illegal *not* to celebrate the date of Guy Fawkes's arrest; while the second, still in effect, says it is actually only permissible to go door to door collecting 'a penny for the guy' with the *written* permission of the local Chief Constable of Police.

THE BIG BANG

Detonating weapons and explosives in public places has come to the attention of lawmakers all over the world. In India, for example, it is against the law to 'discharge or fire certain varieties of crackers like atom bomb and rocket which produce a disturbing noise in or near any public place'. But in Chico, California, the authorities have left nothing whatsoever to chance. For according to their statute book which lists a whole range of banned explosive materials, the biggest fine of all, $500, awaits anyone who 'detonates a nuclear weapon within the city limits'.

KNOCKING THE ROCK

The advent of rock 'n' roll in the mid-1950s sent the lawmakers in a number of countries rushing to their statute books in order to try to placate outraged senior citizens complaining about this new craze for 'gut-bucket music'. In Munich, Germany, for instance, the Office for Public Order took exception to young people dancing to rock 'n' roll at local swimming pools. Hence a ban was imposed on the playing of rock at all local pools. The official reason was that it represented a 'threat to hygiene' and would promote sex orgies.

COOLING OFF

Pittsburgh, the eastern American city which has placed a number of curious pieces of legislation on its statute books, introduced one of the most singular only a few years ago. Health officials became worried after a period of extremely hot weather which knocked out air-conditioning systems and fused many electric fans. What concerned them were some of the strange and dangerous methods being used by citizens to keep cool. So apart from issuing advice on how to prevent heat exhaustion, they also added a new ordinance to the rule books prompted by one particular practice. It was now against the law, they said, for anyone to sleep in their refrigerator.

BLIND JUSTICE

The right to bear arms is, of course, enshrined in the American constitution, but this presented a unique predicament for the police force in the town of Ecorse, Michigan, a few years back when one particular application for a gun licence was presented at the station. For nowhere could they find a precedent for preventing the issue of the licence to a ... blind man.

LYNCH LAW

The terrible practice of 'lynch law' in which local citizens took the law into their own hands and hung malefactors whether or not they were guilty, has existed in the United States for over 200 years. One theory suggests the term originated from the extra-legal courts of Colonel Charles Lynch, a Revolutionary soldier, in the 1780s, in settlements where law had not yet been established – and was primarily used in cases of horse stealing and rape. Although lynching is very rare today – the few cases on record are mostly associated with the infamous Ku-Klux-Klan – anti-lynching bills have tended to be blocked in the Deep South where they are viewed as federal interference in state matters.

Consequently, a number of odd laws are still to be found, such as Section 6281 of the Ohio General Code which reads: 'A person assaulted and lynched by a mob may recover from the county in which said assault is made, a sum not exceeding $500.'

WATERY VERDICT

Another curious example of American law at work occurred in Ohio. Some years ago a man named Robert Spears pleaded self-defence to the charge of murdering a man and throwing his body into the Ohio River. Immediately after his acquittal, Spears was re-arrested and charged again. This time under another old ordinance for 'littering the river'.

STAND AND DRIBBLE

The American state of Louisiana has had more than its fair share of bank robberies during its long history. New Orleans had a par-ticularly violent early history, as did Baton Rouge and Shreveport which once reported a record 28 successful robberies in less than a year. This said, it is perhaps not surprising that there should be a wide-ranging selection of laws attempting to cut down these figures. The weirdest of all threatens a lengthy prison sentence for any robber who threatens a teller with . . . a water pistol.

PISTOL PACKING

Duelling has been effectively legislated against in most European countries, while in America quite a few of the laws that were put in place during the days of the old Wild West to prevent gunfights still remain in effect. None, though, is quite as far-reaching as that to be found in the state of Massachusetts. There it is breaking the law for any form of duelling to take place – even where the intention is harmless and the guns are toys.

GUN LAW FOR WOMEN

The struggle for equal rights for women has been given an added impetus in the Somali Republic in Africa. After centuries in which women were very much second-class citizens, a strict new law has been introduced which prevents men from opposing women's rights either orally or in writing. The punishment for 'spreading propaganda against the rights of women' is ... execution by a firing squad.

BATH TIME

The American state of Vermont has been very keen on keeping its citizens clean. In the little town of Barre, for instance, it was for years obligatory for citizens to take at least one bath every week, with Saturday night being the specified time. Bathers were in danger of breaking the law, however, if they fell asleep while in the tub. In Ohio such cleanliness was apparently frowned upon: for in the small community of Piqua, a local ruling insisted that no one should take a bath before 10 pm; while for many years in the town of Canton there was a local ordinance which prevented anyone from even owning a bathtub.

HAIRY SITUATION

Long hair has been outlawed in the African country of Tanzania where a recent official ruling declared that any man found with hair longer than two inches in length would be liable to an instant haircut and four strokes of the cane. Women, on the other hand, were likely to be similarly punished if found wearing excessive make-up or, worse still, a wig.

GOATEE BAN

In 1870 the city fathers in Boston, Massachusetts, decided to impose a most unusual law on any citizen who chose to wear a goatee beard. Whether this imposition was because they disliked the upper lip adornment or just thought it might be a useful means of raising taxes is not clear – but the fact remains that it is still forbidden to sport a goatee unless the wearer has paid a special licence fee.

STOP THIEF

Hope springs eternal in the hearts of many legislators that they can appeal to people's good nature in the battle against crime. There are few better examples of this than a law enshrined in the law offices at Tacoma in Washington, USA, site of the historic trading post, Fort Nisqually. For in an attempt to stop wrong-doers entering the area, the city fathers entered the following

legislation in their records only 25 years ago: 'It is mandatory for a motorist with criminal intentions to stop at the city limit and telephone the chief of police as he is entering the town.'

BAREFOOT IN THE STREET

The legislators of the great Texan city of Austin many years ago set about improving the appearance of their citizens by introducing a number of laws about suitable dress. Women, they decreed, should wear dresses that covered them to within at least two inches of their feet, while no man should appear in public wearing only his vest. More curious still, neither sex was permitted to walk along the streets barefoot unless they had previously obtained a permit costing $5 from the mayor's office.

SLEEPING BIN

The small west Texas town of Lubbock has two claims to fame. Firstly, it was the birthplace of the great rock 'n' roll star, Buddy Holly and, secondly, it has a strange and very unusual law concerning garbage bins. This requires the waste-disposal operatives working in the city to report anyone they find breaking it. The ordinance says that no person is allowed to sleep in a trash can – and that still holds good even if the receptacle is empty.

HONOUR THE BARD

William Shakespeare, the famous Bard of Stratford-on-Avon, was probably not aware that his ancient profession had long been protected from abuse by a law that is still in existence today. This stipulates that 'no one may insult the king's bard' – those that do, according to the wording of the original document, face a fine of 'eight pence and six cows'.

SNORING ZONE

The city of Cambridge in Massachusetts, USA, is famous not only for its association with the great university town of the same name, but also for having instituted a law about snoring. This perennial complaint of wives against their husbands, and neighbour against neighbour, reached such a pitch in the early years of the nineteenth century, that the city fathers were forced to take action. Though accepting that it would not be possible to place an actual ban on this natural function, they did insert into the local ordinances a rule that 'snoring is not permitted within the boundaries of Cambridge unless the bedroom windows wherein the snorer lies are curtained and securely locked'.

BIG BROTHER

Bureaucrats in the North Yemen government were recently informed that they were about to be stripped of their titles as another step towards a more equal society. An official ruling was sent to every employee which read as follows: 'All official titles used in correspondence, addresses, mass media and in official quarters will be completely abolished to be replaced by the word 'Brother' at all levels.' What gave the normally sombre Yemeni officials a smile was the way in which this directive was signed: 'By order of Lieutenant Colonel Ibrahim Hamadi, Chairman of the Command Council and Commander-in Chief of the Armed Forces.'

TONGUE TIED

Women in Egypt have to be very careful of their language when out in public. In Cairo, the capital, it is against the law for any female to use bad language – especially within the hearing of men. According to the rules, an overheard curse can land a female in jail for a week, while if she repeatedly swears at any male or group of men she risks imprisonment for up to six months. At least this is an improvement on an earlier version of the same law which decreed that a swearing woman would have her tongue cut out.

WITCH POWER

The ancient superstition of witchcraft is banned by law in the African country of Zambia and anyone caught practising the art can be jailed for between three and six months depending on the type of black magic they have been using. The ruling applies to men as well as women and, in a recent case, a Zambian wife was given the full six months after confessing that she had eaten seven of her nine children in order to increase her powers. The woman claimed that she could now fly and also possessed the ability to turn ordinary people into midgets.

TO CAP IT ALL

With all the different kinds of hats and caps worn by men and women today, it is amusing to find that a specific law was laid down in the town of Secaucus, in New Jersey USA, in 1898 about what could and could not be worn. The social stigma that breaking the law would entail was also clearly spelled out: 'Any person who shall wear in a public place any device or thing attached to his or her head, hair, headgear or hat, which device or thing is capable of lacerating the flesh of any other person with whom it may come in contact and which is not sufficiently guarded against the possibility of so doing, shall be adjudged a disorderly person.'

PENILE SERVITUDE

Valentine's Day 1995 was the chosen day when a retired American naval veteran was able to take advantage of a curious federal rule that allows servicemen to receive full pay and benefits both during and after prison sentences. The sailor underwent a special operation at Jackson, Mississippi, which would have cost him $10,000 but for the fact he had just come out of jail after a four-year sentence and was entitled to all his navy benefits. The charge he had gone to jail for was 'sexually molesting two young girls' and the operation he underwent was . . . a penile implant.

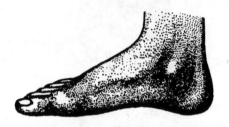

FOOT FETISH

Police in New York, USA, were faced with the difficult choice in 1984 of what to charge a man who persistently broke into the house of two women while they were asleep. His motive was to tickle the feet of a pair of sisters. 'He just likes women's feet,' a puzzled New York detective told the press. 'Some people like other parts of the female body, but he just likes feet.' In the end the foot fetishist was charged with . . . burglary.

NO JOKE

President Ceauşescu of Romania who, until his execution, for over 20 years ran the most oppressive regime in Eastern Europe, was also a man with no sense of humour. He so disliked criticism that he called in the secret police to try to stop people telling jokes about him. Even then he still inadvertently gave his downtrodden population a wry smile by naming the division set up by the dreaded Securitat: 'the Section for Subversive Jokes and Rumours'.

5

ROAD
RUNNERS

The Oddest Highway Codes

Public protests against new motorways and road links have become increasingly commonplace in recent years – especially here in Britain where heritage sites and areas of green belt have come under threat. But in the Channel Island of Guernsey an ancient law still in place allows aggrieved citizens to cry out for justice against such developments – literally.

Ever since the tenth century, an old law known as the *clameur de haro* enables any man or woman living on the island to halt public roadworks until the matter has been settled in court. A recent instance of the law in operation occurred when a householder on Guernsey decided to invoke it to prevent some roadworks going on outside his home. To effect the *clameur* – instituted by the First Duke of Normandy, a man named Rollo, just before his death in the year 932 – the man gathered five witnesses and then fell to his knees in front of the undoubtedly startled workmen. Then, as Rollo's ancient decree stipulated, he recited in French the words: '*Haro, haro, haro* – to my aid, my Lord. I am being wronged!' He followed this by reciting the Lord's Prayer, also in French, to fulfil the requirements of the law.

Whether the five workmen were fully aware of the implications of the act or not, they immediately downed tools and reported the incident to their employers. According to the *clameur*, once the 'cry' has been raised, the disputed action has to be settled during the next 12 months. Any workman who refuses to stop work, though, is apparently liable to 24-hours' imprisonment in the Guernsey Castle dungeon.

Other parts of the world also have their own strange and unlikely codes of highway behaviour which have similarly remained intact on the statute books, as the following pages reveal ...

HORSE BEFORE BIKE

The rapid growth in the popularity of cycling in England after the development of the safety bicycle in 1885 soon presented local authorities with new problems on the roads. In the county of Middlesex on the outskirts of London the frequent encounters between cyclists and horse-drawn carriages resulted in angry exchanges when pedal power swept past horse power, often frightening the animals. The authorities therefore drew up a ruling that cyclists should either dismount when a horse-drawn vehicle approached or, alternatively, if they wanted to pass 'inquire politely of the carriage driver for permission to overtake'.

TUNED OUT

The city fathers of Woodbridge, in New Jersey USA, have a unique claim to fame as the lawmakers who dislike popular music. In 1984 they made it an offence for anyone to walk, jog, ride a cycle or motorcycle, or even drive a car while listening to music as this constituted a danger. Specifically, they decreed that it was an offence punishable by a fine for anyone to be caught wearing personal stereo headphones.

CHICKEN OF THE ROAD

Everyone has heard the phrase: Why did the chicken cross the road? In the tiny community of Quitman in Georgia, USA, this has a special meaning because just over a hundred years ago the local officials banned all chickens from 'crossing any road within the city limits'.

JUST THE TICKET

Traffic wardens in Britain often have to face the abuse of the general public with only the normal laws of society to protect them. Not so in the United States, and especially in New Jersey where the local law authorities laid down rules some years ago that their officers had to be treated with due respect or offenders would face stiff fines. Perhaps the most curious of the laws is that it is an offence to even frown at a policeman when he is giving you a ticket.

FINE LIMITS

Not everyone gets furious when they return to find a traffic warden has given them a ticket for exceeding their parking limit. One motorist in Oklahoma, USA, threw his arms around a pretty warden about to put a fine on his vehicle and kissed her. It didn't get him off the fine, though – instead he was fined an extra $200! Probably the most daunting place to risk a parking fine is Tokyo, Japan. For there the cost of an illegal overnight park is ...£900.

RED LIGHT BRIGADE

The old rule that motor vehicles in the British Isles must be preceded by a man carrying a red flag to warn people of its approach has long been deleted from the statute books – but there is still one corner of the world where the same principle applies. This is in the little American town of Pleasantville, Iowa, where a 90-year-old piece of legislation orders all motorists who pass through the town after nightfall to be preceded 'by a herald carrying a bright red lantern'.

FRIGHTENING HORSES

The lawmakers of the state of Pennsylvania were obviously animal lovers who nurtured serious concern about the effects that the newfangled invention called the motor car might have on livestock. And so they wrote specific guidelines into the rule books for drivers in 1895 – and there they have remained. Two of the laws, in particular, would seem impossible to enforce today.

Statute 10 (b) states: 'Any motorist driving along a country road at night must stop every mile and send up a rocket signal, wait ten minutes for the roads to be cleared of livestock, and then continue.'

And Statue 18 (g) adds: 'Any motorist who sights a team of horses coming towards him must pull well off the road, cover his motor vehicle with a blanket or piece of canvas that blends with the countryside, and let the horses pass. If the horses appear skittish, the motorist must take his car apart, piece by piece, and hide it behind the nearest bushes where it must remain until the animals have passed by.'

FROM THE HORSE'S MOUTH

One of the most remarkable provisos that enables a motorist to park his car for longer than the statutory period of two hours, still exists in the city of Milwaukee, Wisconsin – famous since the mid-1850s as a meat-packing and brewing centre. The city was for years dependent for the success of its commerce on horse-drawn vehicles, which is what has given illegally parked modern drivers a loophole through which to escape a fine. For, according to an ordinance brought into effect in 1864, any vehicle may be left parked in the streets of Milwaukee for over two hours – just as long as it is hitched to a horse.

TAIL LIGHTS

The term 'tail lights' has a special meaning in the town of Berea in the middle of the great American horse-rearing state of Kentucky. For about 90 years ago, in order to avoid accidents at night between riders and the drivers of motor cars, the local authorities laid down the law that no horse may be ridden on the highway, 'unless the animal has secured to its hind quarters a bright red light'. Some law books have claimed that the familiar red rear lights on modern cars actually evolved from this curious and unique piece of legislation.

BATHING SUITS

In these days of bikinis, topless bathing and an increasing number of nudist beaches, the American state of Kentucky still enshrines one old law about female bathing attire which combines a wry common sense with the ridiculous. 'No female shall appear in a bathing suit on any highway within this state,' it declares, 'unless she be escorted by at least two officers of the law or unless she is armed with a club.'

The legislators were unable to let matters rest there, however, for a year later an amendment was written into the state's lawbook which seems even more bizarre: 'The provisions of this statute shall not apply to females weighing less than 90 pounds nor exceeding 200 pounds. Nor shall it apply to female horses.'

BUMMER STICKERS

Car window and bumper stickers are popular with motorists all over the world – the majority declaring nothing more alarming than the name of the couple riding inside or perhaps their love for some far-flung town or country. Only rarely have obscene stickers been reported on vehicles and in only one place are they specifically banned by law. This is in the southern US city of Baton Rouge on the east bank of the Mississippi River in Louisiana. The legislation introduced five years ago is amusingly specific: 'No person shall operate a motor vehicle upon a public road or highway when that motor vehicle displays whether by sticker, sign or painting, any of the following words that are lettered or written in a type or size greater than one-eighth of an inch in height or width: 1. shit, 2. fuck, 3. cunt, 4. tits, 5. piss, 6. cocksucker, and 7. any other word that is a compound or combination of any of these.'

DRIVING TEST

When a new compulsory driving test complete with a written examination was introduced in Italy in 1993, Rafaele Costa, the Minister of Transport, offered to sit the test to prove how easy it was. He failed. Afterwards, the Minister – who had been driving legally for many years – agreed that the questions on the paper were 'a bit obscure'.

FATAL ACCIDENTS

The legislators who drew up the laws concerning motor-car accidents in the American state of Oklahoma were still dealing with the novelty of this new form of transport in the form of inexpensive Fords, Chevrolets and Dodges, when they wrote the rules during the early years of this century. But still these men managed inadvertently to put the following paragraph into the statute book where it remained untouched and a source of amusement for many years:

'The driver of any vehicle involved in an accident resulting in death shall immediately stop and give his name and address to the person struck.'

WHISTLE STOP

Burlington Arcade, a row of exclusive shops just off Piccadilly in the heart of London's West End, is protected from bad behaviour by a unique set of Regency street laws which have remained in force since the precinct was built in 1818. Because it remains private property, two beadles (uniformed commissionaires) still patrol the arcade to make sure members of the public do not 'walk hurriedly, behave boisterously, sing or whistle'. Only one of the original rules has been relaxed to help those who enter the arcade: nowadays it is no longer forbidden to carry a parcel.

BEARDED DRIVERS

The city of Montreal has a long-standing law on its books that motorists may not shave while driving a car on a public highway. As this rule was introduced before the invention of the electric razor it is hard to imagine anyone motoring along with a face covered in shaving foam trying to manipulate a cut-throat razor. The same city also bans the carrying of liquor in cars. Drunken shavers beware!

HAND STANDS

Traffic regulations have always been rigorously enforced in Hartford, Connecticut, the thriving American city on the busy highway between New Haven and Springfield. But there were some people who thought the legislators had gone a little too far when they introduced a new ruling a few years ago that made it against the law for any person to 'walk across the street on their hands'.

CUSHIONED RIDE

There is a danger of prosecution in the American city of Seattle for any girl travelling on the city's normally crowded transport system who accepts a seat on a man's lap. The legislation forbidding this practice was introduced when horse-drawn carriages were the most popular form of transport, but the ruling has remained in force with the coming of the transit bus and underground railway. Curiously, the man himself is not liable to a possible six-month jail sentence – only the girl.

There is, though, one way of getting round this unusual piece of legislation. For the act is perfectly permissible as long as there is a pillow on the man's lap.

BATH-CHAIR BRIGADE

A law is still on the statute books of the city of London governing certain forms of transport in the St James's and Green Park areas in the heart of the metropolis. This was introduced in the late Victorian era and one section specifically refers to Bath chairs – for years the favourite conveyance of wealthy elderly citizens. It threatens a fine to those involved 'if Bath chairs are pushed three abreast'.

HEARSE VERSE

A number of American state authorities are trying to curb

drunken driving by the ingenious use of advertising. In Marshall County, Oklahoma, any convicted driver is forced to place an advertisement in the local paper 'apologizing' for his misdemeanour. In several other states, roadside signs are being erected in a number of prominent locations alongside busy highways – paid for by the fines exacted from drunken drivers. The first of these to be put up said in letters several feet high:

> Drinking drivers, nothing worse.
> They put the quart before the hearse.

WALK THE LINE

In Turkey, the authorities have introduced a novel way of trying to cure drunken driving. It's a variation on the old idea of getting drunks to walk along a straight line – only in this case Turkish men charged with the offence are driven 20 miles out into the countryside and put down by the side of the road. They are then forced to walk back every step of the way to town with a police escort for company.

SOBER SPEED

El Dorado, the oil centre of Arkansas, USA, had plenty of bad behaviour to cope with during the boom years early this century. Fortunes were made and lost, and the city fathers were required to devise a number of special rules to control lawlessness. Reckless driving was prominent among these, a fact that is enshrined in the following peculiar 1907 law: 'Speed upon country roads will be limited to ten miles an hour unless the motorist sees an officer who does not appear to have had a drink in thirty days, in which case the driver will be permitted to make what speed he can.'

CLOTHED IN INNOCENCE

Traffic offences have quite different consequences for husbands and wives in the American city of Omaha, Nebraska. For, some years ago, as an ingenious new deterrent aimed at men who repeatedly appeared in court on charges of bad driving, the city fathers introduced a statute which ruled that every summons would, in addition to paying a fine, require the husband to buy his wife a new set of clothes! And the cost of these clothes was to be exactly the same as the fine imposed upon him.

DOUBLE VISION

The Swiss have always been very proud of their roads and their low record of motoring accidents. The country was one of the first to introduce mandatory seatbelts and also make it illegal for children under the age of 12 to ride in the front seat of a car. This attention to detail has even gone as far as to deal with drivers who wear spectacles – because they are now required by law to carry an extra pair in the car at all times in case of loss or damage to those being worn.

DOOR MATTERS

The provincial towns of England are all still governed by an old law which makes it illegal for anyone to 'beat any carpet, rug or mat in the street' after 8 am. This rule has also crossed the Atlantic in various forms. In San Francisco, California, for instance, no rug may be cleaned in the street except between the hours of 12 midnight and 8 am; while in Port Jervis, New York, all householders are prohibited from spreading a carpet or rug in the street to clean it at any time.

WATERLOGGED

Even off the highway, on water there are still some strange laws on the statute books. In the American state of Tennessee, for instance, the captains and engineers of steamboats are not allowed to race their boats against one another. This 90-year-old piece of legislation, which was no doubt brought in after a number of such competitions had occurred as rivals tried to snatch each other's customers, carries a fine of $500 or six months in jail. If one of the skippers happens to burst his boiler or causes his steamboat to break down, then he can face a prison sentence of two years.

RAILWAY CROSSINGS

It was in Waco, the Texas city whose name used to raise a smile until the terrible fire that took the lives of so many religious cult members in 1993, that a piece of legislation concerning the railroad was put into the state lawbooks in the middle of the nineteenth century. Whether or not the lawmakers were aware of the nonsense of their terminology, this was what they wrote: 'When two railroad trains meet at a crossing, each shall stop and neither shall proceed until the other has passed.'

6

$\mathfrak{S}$INK OR $\mathfrak{S}$WIM

Outlandish Rules Of Sport

Undoubtedly the most curious 'sport' to have been developed in recent years is Dwarf Throwing. Practised mainly in Australia – where it is said to have originated in the late 1980s – and parts of the USA, the event consists of competitors swinging the little people twice backwards and forwards before hurling them as far as they can on to a pile of mats. The dwarfs themselves wear helmets as well as padded jackets fitted with handles which enable the competitors to grasp them securely.

Despite statements from the dwarfs that they enjoy the fun as much as the hurlers, and none has actually been injured during the games, four American states have recently brought in legislation to outlaw the event: New York, New Jersey, Illinois and Florida. In introducing the new laws, state legislators said with political correctness that they believed the practice 'violated the civil rights of little people'.

This ruling notwithstanding, dwarf hurling still goes on in a number of places – with contestants attempting to beat the present record throw of 16 feet. Recently, a bowling-alley version of the event has also been introduced in which competitors push dwarfs standing on skateboards to try to knock down the ten pins.

Controversial though this 'sport' certainly is – it is also only one example of what happens when the law starts playing games...

VERTICALLY CHALLENGED PURSUERS

In a politically correct piece of legislation introduced into the statute books of the American state of Louisiana in 1992, a law was passed to ensure that no group of sportsmen were denied access to any of the local sporting facilities. Specifically, the rule allowed for 'the hunting of deer by dwarfs armed with crossbows'.

WHO'S THE JACKASS?

During the pioneer days in the American state of Ohio, jackass racing was a popular sport among the settlers who considered their horses too important in their everyday lives to risk in races. When disputes broke out among spectators and owners at a number of these events, the legislators moved in to establish new guidelines. Among these was the ruling that the maximum speed at which a jackass could be ridden was six miles per hour, while it was illegal to incite one of the creatures to race if it remained stubbornly at the starting post 'by striking or kicking the beast, or lighting a fire beneath its belly'.

NO YO-YO

Memphis, in Tennessee, is famous all over the world as the place where Elvis Presley lived for much of his life. Today his home, Graceland, attracts visitors of all ages from all over the world. Yet this is a town where children have to be careful what they play with – because an ordinance brought in by the Memphis Council recently has banned all children from playing with yo-yos on Sundays.

FISHY TALES

Those sportsmen who enjoy fishing will find themselves in something of a quandary when visiting Salt Lake City, the famous Mormon settlement in Utah. For here the law bans fishing on Sundays and also says it is forbidden to give fish away on the Sabbath – even if it were possible to catch them! Some restaurants in the state will not even serve fish on this day because of an old ordinance that the people should only eat meat on the Sabbath.

SLINGS AND ARROWS

Muhammad Ali, the former world heavyweight champion boxer, who was raised in the town of Louisville in Kentucky, once related a strange law he actually saw in operation on the outskirts of the city. He was out fishing one day and noticed another boy with a bow leaning over the water. A river warden who came onto the scene immediately warned the lad off. The reason, Ali learned later, was that an old local ordinance specifically prohibited the killing of fish with a bow and arrow.

WATER FASHIONS

Swimmers in Portland, Oregon, the major American freshwater port, are still bound by an odd piece of legislation which has been on the statute books since the early years of this century. Under an ordinance entitled, 'Bathing Without Suitable Dress', is the following ruling: 'It shall be unlawful to bathe in the waters of the Willamette River, or in the waters of any lake, slough or creek within the corporate limits of the City of Portland between the hours of 6 am and 8.30 pm without wearing a suitable dress, which shall cover the body from the neck to the knees, and no person while so attired in said bathing suit or otherwise, shall unnecessarily expose himself to the public view.'

ROLLED OVER

Roller skating, now such a popular sport in rinks throughout Britain, Europe and America, has prompted some strange laws. In Frankfurt, Germany, for instance, it is forbidden to skate more than 50 mph on any rink – and this is the self-same country that permits unlimited speeds for motor cars on its *autobahns* – while in Troyes, France, in the heart of champagne country it is illegal to roller skate after drinking. The toughest rule of all is to be found in the aptly named town of Moscow in Idaho, USA, where roller skating is banned altogether.

SKATING ON THIN ICE

The profession of skating instructor is not without its dangers for any man in the state of Ohio, USA. According to an ordinance which has been on the statute books of this part of America since the turn of the century, it is a felony for a skating teacher to 'attempt to seduce any female student' whether she is on the ice or off it.

WHALE OF A TIME

The laws covering shooting in America are many and varied, but probably the strangest of all relate to the whale. Several states have done their best to preserve this endangered species, though their concern is perhaps a little inappropriate considering their locations. Ohio, for instance, has enacted a statute which forbids whale fishing in any of its 'streams, rivers or lakes on a Sunday'; while in Oklahoma it is against the law to fish for them on any day of the week in any of its inland waterways! Curiously, in California it is prohibited to shoot any game from a car or aeroplane ... except a whale.

NO DUCKING

Duck hunting is another popular sport in many states of America. But according to an old federal law passed in 1893 one group of people are not allowed to pursue this sport anywhere in the nation – though for reasons which are a complete mystery – postmen.

HIGH NOON IN LA

A sporting law which is still on the statute books in Los Angeles, California, reads more like the script for an old movie than a piece of legislation. This states that no form of hunting may take place while riding on the city's transport system. The ruling was made during the early years of this century and specifies that a heavy fine may be imposed upon anyone who pulls a gun or rifle and attempts 'to shoot a hare or jack-rabbit from any trolley car in transit in the city streets'.

FLYING HIGH

Eccentric Californian balloonist Larry Walters caused a major aerial drama a few years ago when he was spotted at 16,000 feet by a passing jet airline pilot. What really startled the aircraft crew and their passengers who watched the balloonist flying over Fresno was the fact he was sitting on a garden chair suspended under 45 weather balloons! When Walters finally became too cold, he shot a number of the balloons with an air rifle and descended safely to the ground. There the police who were awaiting him were completely unable to find any charge to level at the man who had put the entire state on alert. 'Even if he had a pilot's licence,' a law official grumbled, 'we would have suspended it – but he didn't.'

KITES DOWN

The sport of kite flying, which probably originated in ancient China, has not been very popular with a number of English local authorities over the years. In some neighbourhoods the sport is banned on Sundays, while in other places – such as London, Manchester and Birmingham – it is illegal to fly a kite in the street at any time.

SKY-DIVING BAN

Any young woman who wants to take up the sport of sky-diving or parachuting in the American state of Florida had better avoid doing it on a Sunday. Because a law on the statue books, which was passed a few years after the first parachute drop from an aircraft took place in 1912, specifically bans unmarried females from parachuting on that day of the week. The law is a little vague as to whether a married woman can follow this pastime, however, but for the single girl the law threatens a fine or even a jail sentence.

ONE NUL

Women's football is now a very popular sport in Britain, not to mention a number of other countries including France, Germany and the United States. By a curious twist of fate (or was it?), the very year that British women were given the right to vote – 1921 – the Football Association, the sport's governing body, banned ladies' soccer. Indeed, they were not officially allowed back on to the pitch until 1970.

NEVER ON A SUNDAY

Football matches, boxing and wrestling contests and similar sporting events are actually banned from being played before paying crowds in England on Sundays under the Entertainments Act of 1780 which is still in force, although several sections of it have been amended and others are, frankly, just ignored. It is the taking of entrance money at such events that brought the law

down on them originally. Interestingly, another even earlier Sunday ban from the year 1652 has only just been repealed – seemingly permitting what had previously been illegal: 'Bear-baiting, bull-baiting, and all other unlawful pastimes.'

VICTORY BOOB

There have probably been few more unusual charges than the one of 'trespass' levelled at a topless go-go dancer in April 1985. The girl, Morgana Roberts, was also accused of pitch invasion at a football game in Houston, Texas, when she appeared to run on to the pitch to kiss some of the victorious players. Miss Roberts, who has a 60-inch bust, said she did not intend to go on to the playing area, but leaned forward from her first-row seat to get a better view and fell over the railings. Defending the dancer in court, her lawyer said, 'Seven out of ten times if you lean her over a rail she topples over. Anyone who knows anything about the law of gravity will understand that.'

NO GOAL

If an old statute recorded in the mayor's office in Tucson, Arizona, was ever taken seriously then the local university football team would be unbeatable. For it forbids the scoring of goals and threatens a jail sentence of three months or a fine of $300 to any outsider – or team – who does so. The ruling, which dates from around the year 1891 when the university was opened, reads: 'It shall be unlawful for any visiting football team or player to carry, convey, tote, kick, throw, pass or otherwise transport or propel any inflated pigskin across the University of Arizona goal line or score a safety within the confines of the City of Tucson, County of Pima, State of Arizona.'

A LOAD OF BOULES

Curiously, the popular French sport of boules has always been frowned upon as a pastime for small boys in the town of Saverdun not far from the French border with Spain. Years ago, the local authority banned boys under the age of eight from playing the game because they felt it would encourage them to gamble. Those who drew up the rule clearly did not think that girls of the same age might fall victim to the same temptation because they are not mentioned at all.

BULL OF RIGHTS

A number of old sporting events are still listed as being prohibited on the statute books of America's seat of government, Washington, DC. These include bear baiting, cock fighting and men boxing bulls.

UGLY MUGS

The sport of wrestling in California, USA, might be a very different event today if an old ruling from the last century were ever enforced. Worried, apparently, that an excess of 'grimacing and pulling of ugly faces' might affect the result of bouts, the state legislator ruled that all such facial contortions were unlawful and should be prohibited by referees – even to the extent of declaring matches void. Where would the sport be without them!

GETTING TO GRIPS

For many years female wrestling was banned in Germany as it was considered by the authorities that it was not in keeping with female dignity. Recently, however, this ruling has been relaxed – although now no woman is allowed to throw her opponent out of the ring without running the risk of incurring a heavy fine.

KNOCKING THE SPOTS OFF

The American state of Alabama, which briefly belonged to Great Britain before being ceded to the US in 1783, was where the people of the nation were first introduced to the European game of dominoes. Perhaps it was this association with the past that surprisingly caused the state legislature to introduce a ban on the game in 1928. This bizarre ruling under Section 5539 which has never been repealed states: 'Any person who engages in domino playing on Sunday... must be fined.'

GAMBLING BLUFFS

Gambling has come under close scrutiny from the lawmakers in New Hampshire, USA – particularly those gamblers who lose all their money. During the last century a law was introduced under the Public Decency Act which may have saved the embarrassment of big losers but certainly did not please those to whom they owed money. For the legislation declared that it was illegal for a gambler to 'pawn the clothes from his back' in order to settle his debts. Some writers have suggested that it may have been this law that gave rise to the expression, 'taking the clothes from his back'.

EXPLOSIVE STAKES

Card playing has often brought tempers to the boil and provoked angry situations between gamblers. In London, a law is still on record which may well have been drawn up originally for fear of the actions people who were caught up in the emotion of such games might resort to afterwards. This says that it is illegal for any person to possess a pack of cards who 'lives within a mile of any arsenal or store for explosives'.

STRIP POKER

There is one place in the world where the popular card game strip poker has special meaning – although it has never been played legally – and that is the small community of Schulter in Oklahoma, USA. For here, many years ago, the local authority in its wisdom decreed that no female should take part in any game of chance while dressed in revealing clothing, wrapped in a blanket or towel, or in the nude.

7

THE LAW IS AN ASS

Some Unlikely Animal Cases

Few new laws can have been introduced in recent years that were stranger or generated more headlines than the ordinance made by the city council of Charleston in South Carolina, USA, in December 1975, which ordered that all horses were to wear nappies in public! This law had been added to the statute books because, it was said, of increasing complaints about horse droppings on the city streets. The lawmakers' solution to this undeniably noxious problem was greeted with a mixture of hilarity and derision all over the world.

The day on which the law came into force produced a string of stories for the press. Several carriage men agreed to abide by it and duly paraded their horses clad in diapers made of light canvas in every shape and colour. Others resented the idea – in particular those drivers taking carriage loads of tourists around the city. To these men, the bizarre sight of a horse in nappies would drive away customers. One such owner, convicted that same morning of 'riding or driving a naked horse', was fined the maximum penalty of $100. The law also provided for 30 days' imprisonment for persistent offenders – drivers, that is, and not horses.

According to another local carriage driver, the animals were also as resentful of the new ordinance as their owners. 'Horses don't particularly care for their diapers,' he grumbled. Other animals, too, have felt the dumb weight of human law for a good many years...

MULE TRAILS

A similar attempt to clean up the streets was introduced into the small Brazilian town of Angra Dos Reis in 1986. The mayor decreed that it was the dozens of mules who passed through the community each day who were responsible for the mess in the streets and announced that in future all the animals must wear nappies. The result was an immediate furore: with the mule owners claiming they faced going out of business and the local police chief resigning 'because the law is impossible to enforce'. The stubbornness of both parties was finally resolved ... in favour of the mules.

ANIMAL CAPERS

In the Middle Ages, animals were apparently quite frequently – and lawfully – tried in court for a whole range of crimes from causing disease to offending delicate human sensibilities by mating on Sundays. The tradition continues in certain parts of the world today such as Tanzania, where a goat was brought before a court in the south-eastern town of Mtwara in January 1992. The animal was charged with illegally grazing on a private farm and promptly jailed for seven days. Another goat in nearby Kenya also fell foul of a similar law in February 1993. This animal, however, found the paper money which a fruit seller had collected more tasty than his normal fare and was brought before the court for swallowing the sum of 150 shillings. The goat got two days' incarceration – and no doubt a stern warning to stick to his usual diet in future.

PET BIRTH CONTROL

The American state of California is renowned for its weird laws – but there is probably none stranger than the ordinance agreed in Ventura County in 1986. This was issued by the Animal Regulation Committee and ordered that sex between domestic animals 'was only to be permitted within the boundaries of this county on purchasing a duly authorized permit'. Until the citizens of Ventura have paid their $10 for this permit, the committee's statement said, they are legally bound to keep their lustful pets apart.

THE JUNGLE BOOK

The lawmakers in Los Angeles, California, have also taken no chances about the keeping of unlikely pets by local residents. According to Ordinance Number 75169, 'It shall be unlawful for any person to have, keep or maintain, or cause to permit to be had, kept or maintained, or to have in possession or under control within the City of Los Angeles, any elephant, bear, lion, tiger, leopard, hippopotamus or rhinoceros.'

ONE WAY WALKIES

Going up a one-way street the wrong way is bad enough for motorists, but on the Channel Island of Guernsey it can also get the owners of animals into trouble and make them liable for a hefty fine. Here the traffic regulations on one-way streets not only apply to anyone in charge of a vehicle, but also any 'horse, bovine animal, ass, mule, sheep, pig, goat or dog'. Across the other side of the Atlantic in the town of Shawnee, Oklahoma, the city fathers some years ago took exception to dogs being seen in groups and introduced the following strange local law: 'When three or more dogs congregate on any private property without the consent of the owner or occupant and annoy such owners or occupants then this shall constitute a nuisance and make the owners of the said dogs liable to a fine.' The only way round this law is, apparently, to get a written permit from the mayor.

TONGUE TIED

One small community that has gone to the most extraordinary lengths to ensure the well-being of its canine population is a place with the apt name of Normal in the American state of Oklahoma. There are, in fact, several ordinances still in force there relating to dogs – including one that forbids any citizen to give a lighted cigar to his pet. This was probably passed over a century ago, but an even older law on Normal's statute book threatens a fine or even a period in prison for 'making an ugly face' at a dog.

ON THE LEASH

The lawmakers at Arvada, a little community tucked away in the heart of the Bighorn Mountains in Colorado, USA, were probably not intending to sound comic when they introduced a couple of ordinances about dogs to their statute books in the early years of the last century.

'No dog shall be in a public place without its master on a leash,' ordinance number 6 declared. Then on the following page of the rulebook, under paragraph 15, was also written: 'If a stray dog is not claimed within 24 hours the owner will be destroyed.'

DOGS' MEAT

Life can hard for dogs in China where an ancient law says that any canine who strays on to the land of another person becomes, in effect, the property of that person. The landowner is then perfectly within his rights to kill and, if he feels like it, eat the animal. In China, dogs – and puppies, in particular – have long been considered a delicacy when properly butchered and cooked.

IN THE KENNEL

The famous British Dog Kennel Club, founded some years ago by a group of London businessmen who were always in trouble with their wives for being late home from work, would probably be delighted by a law that exists in the town of Wallace in Idaho, USA. For whereas the Englishmen drew the name of their club from an old tradition that a male who was constantly upsetting his spouse deserved nothing better than to be made to sleep in the dog's kennel for the night, the authorities of Wallace have specifically prohibited anyone from sleeping in a dog kennel at any time.

THE DOG THAT BARKED

It was the great fictional sleuth Sherlock Holmes who once remarked during a case that the strange thing about the dog during the night was that it didn't bark. In fact, the problem of barking dogs has exercised lawmakers in various parts of the world – but there are few stranger examples of their deliberations than a rule to be found at Collingwood in New Jersey, USA. Here the authorities calculated what they considered to be a reasonable time span when dogs should be prohibited from barking or howling: the hours between 8 pm and 6 am. What they quite forgot to qualify in the wording of the law was whether it was the dog or his master who incurred the $50 fine.

DUMB FRIENDS

Most animal lovers go to a lot of trouble to train their pets – and do so without requiring the help of the law. Yet although many communities have regulations about the control of animals, only one has a specific ruling against training them. This is to be found in the law book of the town of Hartford in Connecticut, USA. Here it is written under a statute passed early in the nineteenth century and never repealed: 'No person within the boundaries of Hartford shall be allowed to teach, or endeavour to try to educate, a dog.'

CAT'S WHISKERS

A long-standing piece of legislation states that every post office in the British Isles is permitted to employ a cat, in order to keep the vermin down. The weekly wages that these feline guardians were entitled to – depending on the estimated size of the rat and mice population – varied from a basic pay of 3s 6d to the top rate for the best mousers of 7s. At the other end of the spectrum is the American state of Colorado which makes it very hard on people with a rodent problem either at work or home. For according to an old statute no one may buy a mousetrap without first obtaining 'a small-game licence issued by the police authorities'.

CAT BELLS

Animal lovers have tried many different methods of trying to prevent their cats from catching birds. But in only one place is it actually breaking the law not to ensure that a moggie is properly equipped to make this as hard as possible – and that's in the town of Longburn near Palmerston North in New Zealand. For the bird-loving local authorities recently introduced a law that states that all cats must be wearing at least three bells when they are out of doors.

NAGGED TO DEATH

Although not many horses are seen in New York these days, there is still a law governing procedures if one should die in the city. It is found in Section 9 of the Sanitary Code and was introduced on to the statute books around the turn of the century. 'If you have a dead horse,' it reads, 'place it in the street at once with a tag giving name and address. If the horse is not removed at twilight, put lights around the properly protected carcass till it is called for.'

HORSE COUGH

For many years there was a local rule in the town of Newmarket – known far and wide as the Headquarters of Racing – which stated that any man or woman blowing their nose violently in the street was breaking the law. A further addition to this said that 'a person or persons going about the streets with a head cold or distemper' was also liable to be fined. The reason for this health-conscious rule had nothing to do with the citizens of Newmarket but was designed to protect the many valuable horses which were in training in the town from catching a disease.

STABLE DANCE

Horses in the town of Burns in Oregon, USA, enjoy a special privilege shared by no other animals in the world. According to an ordinance established when the town was founded in the late eighteenth century, it is perfectly permissible to take a horse into an inn or night spot where entertainment is being provided. There is just one proviso – an admission fee must be paid for the horse.

UGLY HORSES

Perhaps the most curious law of all relating to horses is one operation in the little American town of Wilbur in the state of Washington. About 150 years ago the local lawmakers introduced an ordinance into their rule books which specified that no man or woman should be seen in the streets riding 'an ugly horse'. The definition of 'ugly' was left strangely unspecified, but there was no doubt that anyone who chose to ignore the fact was liable to a $300 fine which could be imposed by an officer of the law while the rider was still seated on his or her luckless nag.

STUBBORN CASE

A promise made by the American government after the American Civil War ended over 130 years ago to give freed slaves '40 acres and a mule' is now the centre of a campaign in the USA whose leaders claim the pledge is now worth almost $200,000 for every black American. This reparation movement has begun withholding taxes and instituting court cases in a number of southern states, arguing in a statement issued in July 1994, 'Our ancestors had every single pay day of their lives stolen so that whites could be unjustly enriched.' Among the prominent campaigners attempting to seek as much as $110 million in damages 'for the enslavement of our ancestors' is Spike Lee, the black film-maker, who has aptly named his production company, 40 Acres and a Mule.

DONKEY'S YEARS

The age of a donkey when it was changing owners exercised the attentions of the lawmakers in the American state of South Carolina at the start of the nineteenth century after a large number of complaints that animals were being sold who were actually older than the ages given by their prior owners. Inquiries revealed that the teeth of the donkeys were being filed to conceal their real age. The result was a ruling that still exists on the South Carolina statute books forbidding 'the use of dentistry on the teeth of mules or horses' to dupe potential buyers.

GOAT FASHION

There are still a number of curious laws relating to goats in the United States. In New England, for example, a goat that bleats on a Sunday outside a church while a service is in progress can, according to an old law, be considered 'an emissary of the devil' and immediately be put down. The poor creature is also the subject of a strange ban in Chaseville, New York. For here on Sundays no goat may be allowed to pull a wagon past a church 'in a ridiculous fashion'. The law is not specific about what constitutes 'ridiculous', but there seems little doubt that any law officer who attempted to make this charge stick would end up playing the goat!

PIG-NAPPED

Pigs roaming loose on land around the Delaware River near Philadelphia in Pennsylvania were once likely to be taken into custody because of a bizarre old law that maintained they were 'a danger to the navigation of shipping'. Officers of the local authority were empowered to capture the animals and hand them over to any poor local family to kill and eat. The only thing that could save a pig's bacon was if it was wearing a yoke around its neck or ring through its nose to indicate to whom it belonged. Then it was the owners who were in for a roasting for allowing the porkers to get free.

COUNTING CHICKENS

In 1954, a Danish poultry farmer used a local ordinance to claim compensation for his hens after some army manoeuvres had taken place near his land. He successfully claimed that the noise of the soldiers on exercise had left his chickens 'shell-shocked'! A newly married British farmer also took advantage of the law recently when he made arrangements while he was away on his honeymoon for his hens to be fed on the rice that had been thrown outside the church at his wedding. By this means he was able, according to a newspaper report, 'to offset all his wedding expenses against tax as the hens were part of the running costs of his farm'.

BEACH-GRAZING

Farmers in Los Angeles County in America recently received information on a newly introduced law about cattle grazing. Henceforth, it said, they were not permitted to graze cows or similar livestock 'on any public beach'. And unlike English seasides where the donkey giving children rides is still a familiar sight, owners in Los Angeles County are now specifically forbidden to take them on to beaches – with a $50 fine awaiting anyone who ignores this curious ordinance.

THE SILENCE OF ROOSTERS

There is a very unusual old ordinance still in force in the town of Oak Park in Illinois, USA, which is famous as the birthplace of the author Ernest Hemingway. 'Papa' knew about this law which he actually wrote of with some amusement in one of his early articles as a journalist working in Canada. Many years before, he said, the lawmakers had ruled that no rooster should be allowed to crow before 6 am – although they offered no advice as to just how their keepers might be able to keep the birds quiet.

CHICKEN LAW

In Italy, a ruling still exists that any woman convicted of a minor offence cannot be sent to prison if she is pregnant. Over the years this has lead to some ingenious methods of escaping the long arm of the law. As recently as March 1986, a housewife from Pescara, who had been convicted of stealing a chicken in 1975 and sentenced to ten months in jail, was once again brought before the magistrates by the local police in order to enforce the judgement. It had not been carried out to date, the court was told, because the woman had become pregnant a total of 14 times to avoid her fate.

DAWN CACKLE

The people of Biddenden in Kent once grew so tired of being woken up early in the morning by the crowing of cockerels that they laid down a local rule which seems more directed at the birds than residents. 'While not wishing to deny these humble creatures of God their right to summon each new dawn,' the record of the townspeople's deliberations says, 'it is hereafter required that upon the sun rising they take themselves to a distance of not less than 200 yards from any place of human habitation before commencing any sound.'

BIRD LAW

The protection of birds is enshrined in many laws both ancient and modern. But in the state of Utah, USA, this was taken to a previously unheard-of degree by the legislature in 1953. That year it was agreed that it was not people or vehicles that had the right of way on all highways within the state boundaries – but the feathered population.

WHO'S A NAUGHTY BOY?

A parrot can be allowed to testify in a court of law according to a case heard in the American city of Santa Rosa, California. Max, a downy old grey bird, who was found near the body of his owner in November 1991, was allegedly in the habit of constantly repeating himself. The defence used this fact about the bird to substantiate the innocence of their client by maintaining that one of the bird's repeated phrases was irrefutable evidence. Ever since the murder, they said, Max had been heard shrieking over and over again, 'Richard, no, no, no!'

In Cologne, Germany, another of these birds also made news in 1993 when a judge was asked to decide whether a man could be slandered by a parrot. The bird had been trained by its owner to abuse his next-door neighbour during a lengthy feud which resulted in the victim suing for defamation. According to a newspaper report of the case, 'One witness claimed that, on demand, the bird flew into the garden to hurl insults.'

WHAT CAN A PELICAN DO?

The pelican enjoys special privileges in the parks of London

thanks to Section 23 of the Royal and Other Parks and Gardens Regulations Act of 1977. According to this, it is forbidden to 'touch a pelican in any of the aforesaid places, except where written permission has already been obtained'. This rather peculiar rule is in stark contrast to the irregular events which occurred in October 1980 when a man was charged with sexually assaulting a pelican on the Greek island of Syros. The bird was actually the mascot of the neighbouring island of Tinos and the man was arrested shortly after its body was found in a public toilet. Police said that a group of enraged islanders attacked the suspect and he had to be taken into custody. A press report noted, 'The body of the pelican will be stuffed and kept on Tinos.'

WHALE OF A TIME

Although whales are occasionally seen in the seas around the British Isles, they are evidently not as frequently found stranded on the nation's beaches as they once were. For in the reign of Edward II (1284–1327) a special statute was introduced to cover what happened to any that became stranded in order to prevent them from turning into a health hazard. By this law they were made the property of the king to dispose of as he saw fit. Ever since the Middle Ages, this prerogative has remained in force, and today the queen is still entitled to her half of the bargain. According to the original statute the head of any stranded whale goes to the king, while the tail is for the queen, 'to provide whalebone for her dresses'.

DRINKS LIKE A FISH

That favourite old party trick of surreptitiously disposing of an unwanted drink by tipping it into a fish tank is actually against the law in the American state of Oklahoma. There has been a law on the statute books for a good many years to the effect that it is an offence punishable by a fine of $10 to 'cause or induce a fish to become intoxicated'.

HEADLESS TALE

The unauthorized use of royal emblems such as the queen's coat of arms or the rampant lion of Scotland on souvenirs can have the most dire consequences. For under a law that was instituted in 1592 and never repealed, death by beheading is the punishment for 'usurping' the royal arms. The Murder (Abolition of Death Penalty) Act abolished capital punishment for everything but treason, piracy on the high seas ... and copying royal emblems. Amongst recent instances of the infringement, the most publicized was a linen merchant who imprinted the Scottish lion on to bedspreads as a souvenir to mark the Scottish football team's achievement in reaching the finals of the World Cup in 1978. He was fined £100 and allowed to keep his head.

LION TAMERS

Lions obviously do not make ideal pets, but at least one local authority has made specific provisions about what its citizens should do if they decided to keep one of these animals at home. The town is called Alderson in Virginia, USA, and there about sixty years ago an ordinance was brought into force which reads: 'No lions shall be allowed to run wild on the streets of this city.' What caused the introduction of this extraordinary rule is now a complete mystery.

WILD PASSIONS

An antiquated law in Iran, which has never been removed from the statute books though it was written several hundred years ago, permits men, if they wish, to have sex with a number of domestic animals including dogs, donkeys and lambs. The rule adds in a footnote that sex with wild animals is not recommended, 'especially with a lioness'.

ELEPHANT WORLD

Disney World in Orlando, Florida, which each year draws millions of tourists of all ages from all over the world, has recently introduced a unique new ordinance. Its subject is elephants which are, of course, used for giving rides and advertising the delights of the huge pleasure complex. But when the animals are being rested, the city fathers decided, this must be done in a proper parking space. And if the elephant is tied to the meter then it must be charged exactly the same parking fee as if it were a car.

BEAR-FACED CHEEK

Back in 1935, a hunter in trouble-torn Yugoslavia instituted a case in Belgrade against a bear which attacked and mauled him while he was out hunting in a forest in central Bosnia. After hearing the evidence and consulting the old statute books, the court found in favour of the hunter and awarded him compensation of the approximate value of £100 on the grounds of 'fear, injury, loss of wages, damage to clothing and hospital and court expenses'. According to a report of the case, 'In the absence of the bear in court, an order was made against the local forestry commission.'

BEAR AWARE

The grizzly bears of Alaska, USA, enjoy a unique immunity from intrusion into their lives by photographers that is denied to human beings. For although this state has permitted the hunting of bears for many years – providing the hunter has a licence – a statute is still in force which decrees that, 'no person may disturb a grizzly bear in order to take its picture'.

THE LAW STINKS

That rather unlovable little creature, the skunk, actually had a group of legislators who fought for its rights in the state of Pennsylvania, USA, in 1979. Worried that the animal might be in danger of extinction because of the determination with which it was being hunted and killed, the lawmakers introduced an 'Act For the Better Protecting Of Skunks'. This made it unlawful to tease or torment skunks or polecats and threatened a fine for anyone who broke the law.

SMOKING BAN

A performing chimpanzee, whose range of tricks included peeing on audiences and swallowing lighted cigars, is believed to have been the reason why the city fathers of South Bend, Indiana, USA, introduced a special ruling into their laws which has never been rescinded. This prohibits 'any monkey, orang-utang, chimpanzee or ape' from smoking in a public place.

UNDERCOVER BEES

A nun was recently charged with smuggling 6,000 European bees into Kenya. The sister of the Greek Orthodox Church said she was bringing the bees into the country to produce beeswax for church candles. Although she disputed the number of bees in her possession – she claimed to have just four queens and about a 100 others – the 'illegal immigrants' were destroyed by the Kenyan authorities who feared they might carry disease. The sister was arrested at Nairobi airport when the sound of the bees' humming was heard by customs officers ... under her habit.

BUTTERFLY HAVEN

The protection of wildlife has achieved many worthwhile objectives and undoubtedly saved a large number of species from extinction. Perhaps, though, nowhere is the law more unusual than in the Pacific Grove community in California, USA. For here it is forbidden to 'kill, disturb or threaten butterflies' or else run the risk of a $500 fine and up to six months in jail.

YOU DIRTY RATS!

In January 1993, a shopkeeper in the town of Busia in Kenya tried to utilize an old law which permitted animals to be tried for crimes. The man walked into the police station with four live rats and demanded that they be arrested for ruining his bread supply. 'I want these rats put in the cells and charged in court for damage,' he said. The officers, finding him to be 'sober and of sound mind', advised the shopkeeper instead to contact the local public health officer.

SPARE THAT MOUSE

Surprising as it may seem, mice enjoy protection under the law in the American town of Cleveland, Ohio. Over the years the town's lawmakers have passed a number of laws about the hunting of animals – and mice feature prominently among them. In fact, it is only legal for a man to hunt and kill one if he has a valid hunting licence!

WORMS' CASTS

Even the humble worm is protected by law in certain parts of Britain. An ancient law dating from 1171 forbids digging worms for bait in a number of coastal areas including Maldon in Essex, where one early-morning digger, caught in the act in 1993, was fined £50, and was informed that he risked a fine of £1,000 if caught again. In the county of Northumberland, there is an even more up-to-date version of this ruling which was introduced in 1968 by the local authority because it was feared that bait diggers might endanger the nesting habits of local birdlife. The language of the statute was in the very best tradition of bizarre laws: 'That the taking, molesting, wilfully disturbing, injuring or killing a living creature, namely a lugworm, is forbidden and as such punishable by a fine.'

UP THE POLE

Of all the curious laws relating to pets, the strangest must surely be the one to be found on the statute books of a place with the impressive name of International Falls in picturesque Minnesota, USA. Here amidst a welter of restrictions relating to horses, cows, sheep and dogs is one that refers to cats. Almost unbelievably, it decrees that 'no cat may be allowed to chase a dog up a telegraph pole'.

PET SEPARATION

The problems occurring when couples separate or get divorced are bad enough where there are children concerned, but in pet-mad America they can be even more acrimonious. In the town of Madison, Wisconsin, the lawmakers have been faced with this problem so many times that a law is now on the statute books. Here joint custody of the animal will not be granted – the pet will be legally awarded to whichever partner was looking after it at the time of the initial separation. And that's final!

8

$\mathfrak{S}$EX $\mathfrak{A}$CTS

The Loopholes Of Love-Making

Where sex is concerned, one very ancient law has been the subject of a great deal of controversy among modern-day scholars: the *droit du seigneur*. For years a part of popular tradition and having long ago captured the imagination of writers such as Cervantes, Voltaire and Tolstoy – as well as being featured in numerous European classics, among them *The Marriage of Figaro* – the *droit du seigneur* sanctioned the lord of the manor taking the virginity of his female serfs.

Some historians, however, believe that this *jus primae noctis* (which literally translates as 'a nobleman's legal right to the bride's first night of marriage') is actually a figment of male fantasy seized upon by randy lords centuries ago to justify their lusting after beautiful peasant girls. Also disputed by this group is another idea from the Middle Ages that after any of his servants got married, a nobleman could call upon the couple to enjoy the bride's 'first fruits'.

The majority of scholars, however, believe the idea *is* based on fact and that it actually originated in the East. There it was designed to protect young males from having to 'venture their most untried and vulnerable part into a woman's place of devils'. For centuries various expedients were in operation to avoid this 'risk' – the most widely used being the defloration of the bride by an older man. It was from this tradition that the *droit du seigneur* evolved, the scholars believe – although some think that for a number of lords endowed with an ugly population it was considered more of a chore than a legal right.

According to one Anglo-Saxon law which is recorded, young girls were also legally bound to pay a *legerwite* to their lords as soon as they got married. This term literally meant 'money for lying down' and was a payment for being deflowered without the lord's permission.

Sex today may have lost some of its more bawdy and colourful remnants from the past – but there have still been plenty of lawyers who have busied themselves laying down the very strangest of laws concerning love-making …

RECIPE FOR SEX

Another ancient French law dating from the Middle Ages was recently cited by the beautiful, blonde manageress of a restaurant in Lille, the northern French city once the capital of Flanders and renowned for its textile manufacturing. What brought Michelle Michel to the attention of the authorities was the fact that the delights of her kitchen were not reserved exclusively for the customers. For while the diners loved her cooking, she was loving her cooks – ten in all whom she allegedly 'forced' to go to bed with her and which resulted in her being accused of sexual misconduct. But Michelle had an answer to the charge: she said she had every right to seduce the young men under an ancient local rule which had never been repealed called 'The Thighs Right'. This permitted any landowner to seduce maidens working on his estate. And what was right for the gander, claimed Mme Michel, was surely also right for the goose!

BRIBERY OR CORRUPTION

British Members of Parliament, a number of whom in recent years have been the subject of sensational newspaper stories alleging impropriety and suggestions of corruption, would no doubt be amused by a revealing piece of legislation contained in a statute book in Virginia, USA. For the heading of this document passed in all seriousness in 1930 would seem to permit elected representatives total freedom for just about any kind of underhand activities. It reads: 'To Prohibit Corrupt Practices or Bribery by Any Person Other Than Candidates.'

COCK AU VAN

The authorities of Detroit, Michigan – known throughout the world as the centre of the motor-car industry – not surprisingly have a string of laws on the statute books concerning automobiles. The strangest of these relates to the delicate matter of couples making love on the back seat of a car. Five years ago this was made legal – as long as the act took place in a vehicle parked on property belonging to either the man or the woman.

HONK 'N' BONK

The quaint little town of Liberty Corner in New Jersey, USA, has a law that completely refutes its name – certainly where love-making is concerned. For if a couple have sex in a car and accidentally sound the horn during their moments of passion, they fall foul of a local law against 'obnoxious activity' and can be hauled before the court and fined. Both partners are considered equally guilty and fined the same amount.

FERTILE FIELDS

Farmers on the beautiful island of Java in Indonesia have a quaint local law which they can invoke if their rice crops are in danger of failing or appear likely to produce a poor yield. For over 300 years this ruling has required that local married couples living within the vicinity of an endangered farm are to forgather there 'once a week as the sun goes down'. Then by what can only be termed as an example of 'sympathetic magic' at work, the men and women are expected to ensure the fertility of the crop, 'by performing intercourse as many times as is within their capabilities'.

BLUE MOVIES

For many years film makers in Hollywood were under a strict code that forbade the use of certain words in scripts – including 'sex', 'wench' and 'madame' and from showing any scenes which might suggest intercourse was about to occur: in bedroom scenes, for example, a man always had to keep at least one foot on the floor. Perhaps the most amusing instruction of all to movie producers was this: 'The expression of a "travelling salesman" must under no circumstance be used in conjunction with any reference to a "farmer's daughter".'

DISORDER IN COURT

In 1984 a new law was introduced into the statute books in Milan, Italy, which ruled that all defendants appearing on charges relating to terrorism were to be placed in separate witness boxes while on trial. This had followed reports that a couple involved in a bomb plot had 'engaged in sexually explicit activity' while evidence was being given in the courtroom. Nine months later, twin boys had been born to the female terrorist, it was added.

CUDDLE PUDDLE

Love-making in ponds and pools is banned in Swaziland, in southern Africa, as result of a 1985 government ruling. Users of the area's famous hot springs pool – known locally as the 'Cuddle Puddle' were warned by the authorities that fines and even imprisonment would be imposed on those caught in the pool breaking the new rule. Prince Khuzulwandle, the minister of Natural Resources, Land Utilization and Energy, said that it had been necessary to bring in the legislation because too many pool users were still ignoring earlier warnings and 'having sexual intercourse under water'.

THE SUNDOWNER

A curious law against love-making at night is still on the statute books in Birmingham. According to a centuries-old ordinance it is illegal for a man and woman to have sex 'on the steps of any church after the sun goes down'. The act constitutes 'disorderly conduct' and can result in a fine of £25. A loophole in this law is that it makes no reference to the same act carried out in daylight!

CUTTING RULE

Chinese law frowns on couples who have more than one child, for it is considered the duty of men and women to look after their aged relatives in preference to raising children. In the Indian state of Uttar Pradesh, however, couples are allowed a little more freedom: though the punishment they face for abusing the law is much harsher. Here any man and women may have up to three offspring, but after that the law says the husband must be sterilized. Any man who attempts to defy this rule is likely to be imprisoned for two years – during which time the vasectomy will be carried out voluntarily or under restraint.

FALL FROM GRACE

Married men looking for an excuse for extra-marital sex need look no further than the island of Cyprus which has had a rather laissez-faire attitude towards certain types of intercourse since the earliest times. Single women, for instance, could offer themselves quite legally as prostitutes in order to raise the money for their dowries. More curious still is an equally ancient rule which permits married men to have sex freely although the conditions which make it legal are as unusual as the language in which it is couched. 'A husband shall be enabled to have sexual intercourse with a woman who is not his wife if, while looking over a parapet or railing, he accidentally stumbles over and falls upon a passing female and thereby effects a accidental union with her. This in all the particulars shall not be considered an unlawful act.'

PIN-UP BAN

The pin-up photograph, which is so familiar throughout the world is actually banned in the Cautin province of Chile. Here pictures of scantily dressed women are outlawed not only in factories and clubs, but even the ordinary householder risks a fine for pinning one up on his wall.

The ruling was brought into force in 1976 by the military governor of the Cautin region who said when issuing details of fines to be imposed on those who disobeyed: 'It is more worthwhile to admire a good landscape than a photograph of a nude woman.'

PEEPING TOMS

There are innumerable laws dealing with Peeping Toms all over
the world. In Krasnoyarsk in Russia, for instance, an old rule
allows any law officer who catches a man who is not fully dressed
when he is peeping to 'beat him soundly' before arresting him. In
North Carolina, USA, only male voyeurs are covered by the law –
a woman there cannot be arrested for doing the same thing
through a man's window if he is undressing inside. And in Texas,
there are now two legal exemptions relating to Peeping Toms – no
male can be charged under law if he is either 'over 50 years of age
or has one eye'.

HIDDEN CHARMS

Nudity is regarded in a very ambivalent way in modern China – as it has been for centuries. In the vast rural areas of that great nation, the law says that a man may look upon the nearly naked body of another man's wife without fear of recrimination. He may not, though, have sex with her without her husband's permission! There is, though, one part of her body that no self-respecting Chinese woman would allow any man other than her husband to gaze upon. It is a part that the law actually permits an outraged husband to kill a nosy culprit for looking at without fear of recrimination: her feet.

PHOTO MODESTY

The American city of Oxford in Ohio is the seat of the famous Western College for women which was founded in 1853. Modern students on the large campus would probably be amused to learn that they are still subject to a hilarious piece of legislation that was put into effect some years before the college was opened and has never been repealed. It states that no woman may undress while standing in front of the picture of a man.

LICENCE FOR SEX

Prostitutes are given considerable leeway to practise the oldest profession in the city of Bologna, Italy, which seems to be living up to its reputation as a strong, free commune earned during the twelfth century when it escaped from papal rule. A girl on the game in the city cannot be arrested even if caught *in flagrante delicto* in a car thanks to a ruling that has been operating for the past 50 years. It permits those who lead 'a scandalous life' to escape prosecution – just as long as they 'drive carefully'.

HOPE FOR THE FUTURE

Because of the terrible effects of venereal disease on the population of the African country of Uganda, an optimistic law was recently introduced to combat the ignorance and embarrassment people evidently felt about contracting the illness. Believing that many people were too ashamed to go to a doctor for help, the authorities decided on introducing a euphemism that would enable anyone to get treatment merely by whispering the words to a medical man. The password they agreed upon was 'Good Hope'.

SEPARATE LIVES

The course of young love has not been made any easier in China where the Communist authorities introduced a new law in 1994 to try to stop couples living together before the official 'marriageable' age. This is 22 for men and 20 for women. The reason for this new statute to prevent couples cohabiting was given in an official announcement: 'in order to tighten population control'.

WINKING LIMIT

The apparently harmless pursuit of winking at a pretty girl is acceptable everywhere except at Ottumwa on the Des Moines River in Iowa, USA. A municipal code enacted around the turn of the century declares that 'It is unlawful for any male person, within the corporate limits of the City of Ottumwa, to wink at any female person with whom he is unacquainted.'

KISSING BAN

The minister of Education in West Bengal, India, was responsible in 1958 for introducing legislation that prevented the showing of films in which kissing scenes occurred. This ruling insisted that any such acts of passion between actors and actresses in Indian or foreign films had to be censored before they were screened in public cinemas. In passing the law, the minister said that the reason for his decision was quite simple. 'The showing of kissing in such films might cause grave harm to society as they would act as a brain softener.'

FLIRTING WITH DANGER

Few visitors to New York, one of the most sophisticated cities in the world, are aware that flirting is actually a crime. A statute has been on the Big Apple's law books since the last century that threatens any man who 'looks unashamedly at a woman' with a fine of $25. For persistent offenders, the rules provide a further punishment in the form of a pair of horse blinkers which the man is compelled to wear, 'so that he may not continue staring indecently upon ladies whenever he is on the city's streets'.

STOCKING TOPS

One tiny corner of the great American state of Texas still looks upon the sight of stockings as something shocking. In the town of Dennison an ordinance was put on the local rule book in the 1920s that any woman who stopped to pull up, straighten or adjust her stockings in a public place or on the street was committing a 'lurid act'. If convicted of this offence, a female might expect to be sentenced to up to a year's imprisonment in the state penitentiary.

BALLROOM GOWNS

Dressing in women's clothing for fancy dress parties may never have been the most popular pastime in the rugged Australian city of Melbourne, but according to an old local rule to do so is actually against the law and could get the culprit arrested and thrown in jail. For about 100 years ago – perhaps following complaints? – the city authorities made it illegal for 'a man to appear in public wearing a strapless gown'.

SHOE SHINE

The big American industrial city of Cleveland, Ohio, has one of the most interesting laws concerning women's shoes. Some years ago the legislators passed a law that prohibited women and girls from wearing patent leather shoes in public. The reason for this ruling was to preserve female modesty, the statute declared. A paragraph in the ordinance explains everything: 'The wearing of such high-gloss footwear may encourage members of the opposite sex to look down and thereby see a reflection of the woman's legs beneath her skirts.'

NIGHT-CLUB PERFORMERS

A group of lawmakers in the American state of Montana – once famous for its lawless ways – went to the other extreme when they introduced several new ordinances relating to the performing arts. The men were making the laws for the town of Helena and paid special attention to the girls who performed in either night clubs or taverns. They must, the law decreed, 'wear no less than three pounds two ounces of clothing at all times'. Curiously, no stipulation was laid down as to how this clothing should look – which caused one quick-thinking entrepreneur to dress his girls in large waist-bustles and very little else.

TOPLESS VIEWS

A bizarre law introduced recently in Sweden concerns photographs taken in coin-operated automatic photographic booths. According to this ruling it is illegal for men and women to take full-frontal nude pictures of themselves. Conversely, it is perfectly all right for either sex to photograph themselves topless or from the waist down.

TIT BITS

A curious loophole in the law governing topless photographs of girls has enabled publishers in Brazil to titillate male readers. For the rule of censorship as it relates to newspapers, magazines and books states that 'no more than one female breast may be shown on any given page'. So side-on views of lovely models are all the rage.

UNDERCOVER WORK

In the city of Los Angeles, USA, a quaint old rule about feminine underwear comes into force every winter. Because of an ordinance made more than a century ago, women are permitted to hang their lingerie out in the open air during the summer months, but once fall arrives they must be hung indoors or else the owner runs the risk of a $100 fine. Law officers are even empowered to remove the offending articles at the time of conviction.

FINGER LICKIN'

One of the oldest tribal laws to be found in the Melanesian Islands off the coast of Australia is still in force at Madang on New Guinea. It concerns adultery and allows a cuckolded husband to legally decapitate his wife's lover when he discovers their infidelity. Before he does this, however, the law also requires that the lover must cut off one of the fingers or toes of the object of his affection, 'and eat it before the assembled tribesmen and their women as a lesson to all'.

TICKLISH PROBLEM

The lawmakers in the American city of Portland, Oregon, found themselves in a ticklish situation a hundred years ago when asked to draft an ordinance about the use of feather dusters. This followed a number of complaints by local wives against their husband for allegedly taking liberties with servant girls: either by tickling them under the chin with their fingers or, more frequently, snatching the girls' feather dusters and using these to tease them. The canny lawmakers – all men, no doubt – came up with a ruling that no women should allow a man to tickle her under the chin with a feather duster. What they didn't ban was the tickling of any other part of the body!

KING-SIZE CUTS

In 1982, the king of Thailand instituted a campaign in Bangkok to cut down on unwanted children by starting a campaign, 'Have a Vasectomy for the King', which was launched on the eve of his fifty-fifth birthday. Over 700 Thais responded to the legislation within a matter of hours – one man later declaring that it was a song, 'I'm Vasectomized', then at number three on the Thai hit parade, which had inspired him.

GOING FOR A SONG

The Chinese authorities have in recent years been conducting a vigorous campaign in the press and on radio against the old practice of selling young women as brides or mistresses. This age-old custom, which was for years perfectly legal in many rural areas where poor families could only make ends meet by bartering unwanted female children, is now the subject of several songs as well as the regular news bulletins which describe it as 'a remnant of feudal times'. Although hundreds of traffickers have been caught and convicted in the most populated province of

Sichuan, the catchy songs are said to have actually led to a revival of the brides-for-sale market in no less than seven others.

BATTLE OF THE SEXES

Female soldiers form an important part of the Taiwanese Army. Three years ago, the defence ministry made a ruling that no woman officer was to be seen in high-heeled shoes – even off duty. The reason for this draconian measure against fashion was simply explained. 'Soldiers in high heels appear more suited for love than war,' a ministry spokesman stated.

BOTTLED UP

An Islamic law in the Sudan forbids the dealing in alcohol and threatens a year in prison or 60 lashes for culprits who are caught. A recent sufferer under this ancient ruling was a Korean shopkeeper who received the sentence of lashing for selling Scotch to several woman and, according to the charge, 'contemplating adultery'.

SOUNDS OF PASSION

Probably the most curious grounds for a divorce were entered in a case heard in an Israeli court in Jerusalem in October 1994. A woman there informed the court that she wanted a separation after four years of married life, 'because my husband makes no groans or noises of passion when we make love'.